THE LISTENER'S GUIDE TO **The Blues**

THE
— LISTENER'S GUIDE —
TO

The
Blues

PETER
GURALNICK

Facts
On File
☑

A Quarto Book

Copyright © by Quarto Marketing Ltd.
and Peter Guralnick

First published in the United States in 1982 by **Facts On File, Inc.**

Library of Congress Cataloging in Publication Data

Guralnick, Peter.
    The listener's guide to blues.
    Includes discographical references.
    1. Blues (Songs, etc.)—History and criticism.
2. Blues (Songs, etc.)—Discography.   I. Title.
ML3521.G87   784.5'3'0015   81-9812
ISBN 0-87196-567-4   AACR2

The Listener's Guide to The Blues
was produced and prepared by Quarto Marketing Ltd.
212 Fifth Avenue, New York, New York 10010

The Listener's Guide Series was conceived
by John Smallwood
Editor: Gene Santoro
Design: Elizabeth Fox
Typesetting: Scarlett Letters, Inc., N.Y.
Printed and bound in the United States
by the Maple-Vail Group

CONTENTS

Introduction: Discovering the Blues

This book is intended as a beginner's guide to the blues. It's meant to play a utilitarian role by providing the interested listener with both a listing and a context. The listing represents a personal selection in which I've tried to be objective, but I've done my best to be open about my biases, too. The context is an attempt to provide a narrative thread in which to set the music. I've tried to make clear the connections and also pay homage to those singers who exist without connections and are to be listened to for the pleasure of their genius alone. I've sought to strike a balance, in other words, between a strictly deterministic view and the Great Man Theory of History. I hope I've done so with common sense and without too much oversimplification, but if I've erred I hope it's been—not too glaringly—on the side of clarity.

I wrote this book because I thought it would be fun—and it was. It's fun making lists, and it's fun passing along your own enthusiasms. I've been listening to the blues myself for over twenty years now, since I was fifteen years old, when my friend, Bob Smith, and I discovered some blues records and devoured Sam Charters's book, *The Country Blues*. As I wrote in *Feel Like Going Home,* my first book: "The blues captured me initially by its directness of impact. I had never known a more searing expression of emotion . . . From my first exposure I found myself enthralled in a way I had never experienced before . . . [It] appealed to something deepseated and permanent in myself, it just sounded right."

It still does. I don't know why today any more than I did then. Bob Palmer wrote that the story of the Delta blues was "an epic as noble and as essentially American as any in our history." Maybe that's it. All I know is that the blues turned me around. At one time it was exotic, at another commonplace; it's been chic, and it's been ignored. Throughout all the changes—and through shifting enthusiasms in other areas, in politics, literature, and music, too—the blues has been a constant for me. The blues was my first (musical) love, and it will very likely be my last.

This book is an attempt, then, like most of what I've written about the blues, to give something back, to steer the reader towards an appreciation of something that's meant a great deal to me. In this case I've tried to cover most of the broad ground, from vaudeville blues to the present day, with some dispassion but without fear of letting my prejudices show. You'll probably recognize the blind spots and dead spots on your own. I haven't tried to disguise them or make it seem as if I'm equally enthusiastic about every record or every artist discussed. These are records with which I've lived for the most part for many years. In some cases I've known them for as long as fifteen or twenty years, and invoking them is a little like summoning up old friends: I feel both proud and challenged to be able to present to you my favorites. The feeling is almost the same as when I first started writing about the blues: a sense of wonder and gratification at simply seeing the names in print.

There have been omissions necessarily. In some cases I've had to cut out records that are personal favorites but are simply too marginal to require introduction to the beginning listener. Some areas of the blues — piano, ragtime, and postwar California — have been given short shrift because they fall outside the particular purview of this study. Length has been a consideration. I've tried to keep availability in mind to a certain extent as well, but records go in and out of print so rapidly that I've simply tried to be guided by common sense. For the most part I've used the most readily comprehensible label designation. For example: at the time that I write there are no Chess records available in the United States. Nonetheless, I've kept the Chess designation, both because I believe that Chess will come back into print under some conglomerate's auspices and because, worldwide, this is the way they are always going to be known. On the other hand, I've avoided Japanese issues simply because their availability is too uncertain. Most of the issues are American, but many (like Charly or Flyright) are not, and the enterprising listener will undoubtedly have to search out even the most common (see Appendix on Where to Buy Blues Records) or apply his imagination to find the same record under different licensing arrangements in other countries. The point is, if you want to collect blues records, you have to have a little bit of the prospector about you.

I hope that my suggestions will lead to your forming your own tastes and drawing your own conclusions. If you follow the format of this book, you should have a good exposure to the blues. It may not move you the way that it has moved me, but I think if you listen you will make some surprising connections. For blues is not as it has often been portrayed: a slow, ponderous, and desolate music that, in a sense, "gives you the blues." In reality, blues is a music of joyful self-expression, most commonly a dance music designed to take away the blues, and if it has occasionally assumed the form of an art music in its seventy-five-year life span, it has far more often served, in the words of St. Louis bluesman Henry Townsend, as "a relief for pressure." The blues is not a form anyway, but a feeling, an expression of human need that has evolved and will continue to evolve. The changes should neither alarm nor enlighten but merely give further proof to blues pianist Otis Spann's dictum that the blues never die but serve, instead, a vital function. As Spann sang,

"When you in trouble blues is a man's best friend/ Blues ain't gonna ask you where you going / And the blues don't care where you been."

SELECTED RECORDINGS

■ **The Story of the Blues (Columbia)**

Put together by blues historian Paul Oliver to illustrate his book of the same name, this is the best overall survey of blues styles and blues evolution—from chants of the Fra-Fra tribesmen to Chicago blues by Johnny Shines and Elmore James. All of the principal trends are here—pre-blues, vaudeville blues, urban and rural variations—all set off by good examples and good sound reproduction. A great starting-off point.

■ **The Rural Blues (RBF: two-record set)**

This set is subtitled "A Study of the Vocal and Instrumental Resources"—and to a large extent that is what it is. It was compiled by Samuel Charters, author of the groundbreaking *The Country Blues,* from commercial issues and field recordings made by Charters in the 1950s. Confined as its title declares to country blues, it divides the various examples into broad categories illustrating "Coarse Vocal Tones," "Deeper Chest Tones," and so on, and sounds more forbidding than it really is. For the one common denominator is that this is all great music, and the listener is guided by Charters's unerring taste through a thicket of blues that includes everything from Papa Charlie Jackson's 1926 debut on blues banjo to Charters's landmark recordings of Furry Lewis and Lightnin' Hopkins in the late 1950s.

■ **The Country Blues (RBF)**

Very much like the above except: 1) it is confined to commercial recordings of the 1920s and 1930s; and 2) unlike **The Rural Blues** it has no didactic axe to grind. Charters put out this record in 1959 to accompany first publication of his book, and it includes such seminal recordings as Blind Lemon Jefferson's "Matchbox Blues," Blind Willie McTell's "Statesboro Blues," the original Cannon's Jug Stompers version of "Walk Right In," along with indispensable cuts by Robert Johnson, Bukka White, Leroy Carr, and Sleepy John Estes. Despite muddy sound, a characteristic of all RBF reissues, and despite a proliferation over the last twenty years of blues reissues that cover much the same ground, I think there could not be a more entrancing introduction to the country blues.

■ **Really! The Country Blues (Origin Jazz Library)**

Almost as much a revelation as Charters's collection when it came out a couple of years later. The purpose of the Origin Jazz Library was to unveil the obscurities who lay behind the blues legends—to reveal Tommy Johnson, Son House, Skip James, and Charley Patton, all blues household names today, as the *real* progenitors of the blues styles popularized by such better-known bluesmen as Robert Johnson, Leroy Carr, and Big Bill Broonzy. To a large extent Origin was successful in their revisionist quest, but you shouldn't think that gravity of purpose has ruled out entertainment value. Instead, there is revealed a sparkling variety of early blues styles, from the irrepressible good humor of Sunny Boy and His

Pals singing "France Blues"to the somber drama of Skip James's "Devil Got My Woman." Just to give you an idea of the state of blues research at the time, the notes on Skip James read as follows: "No details. Said to have been from Louisiana. Was proficient on both guitar and piano. Present whereabouts unknown." A lot of water has passed under the bridge since then, but no greater blues music has surfaced.

■ Conversation With the Blues (English Decca)

An oddball choice, since it is out of print and not made up of music exclusively. Assembled by Paul Oliver from the field research that went into his book of the same title, the record is a collage of monologues (like the book) mixed in with idiomatic field recordings of the music. The result is eloquent talk and expressive music— perhaps not the kind of record that you're going to listen to over and over again but more successful at conveying the spirit of the music than many more conventional collections. Highly recommended, if you can find it.

■ Country Negro Jam Session (Arhoolie)

A rowdy footstomping collection of field recordings made in perfect innocence by folklorist Harry Oster, this captures better than anything else that I can think of the raucous joyful atmosphere of the backwoods country blues. Recorded in a number of rural Louisiana locations by a number of different singers, it is dominated by the heavily strummed guitar of Willie Thomas set off by the antiphonal fiddle of Butch Cage and the rough-edged, garbled, and irrepressible singing of both. Many of the songs will already be familiar from commercial versions by Howlin' Wolf or Willie Cobbs or Barbecue Bob—and undoubtedly this was where the singer learned them. They are transmuted, though, by a sense of place and a sense of engagement, by the supportive cries of the singers' friends and families, by the very palpability of their surroundings, until we can only be grateful for our invitation to enter the artist's home, to take part in his or her good times. A unique process of spiritual transference has taken place. Unhesitatingly, unwaveringly recommended.

—2—

Land Where the Blues Was Born

Tracing the origin of the blues can be a problematic and somewhat theoretical venture because the blues is an oral, not a written, tradition, in which the need for maintaining a documented genealogy has never been exactly paramount. Nonetheless, a number of reasonable theories have been suggested, all of which center on the interaction of African culture and the condition of slavery in the New World. A good number of vestiges of this African tradition can be found in the blues to this day—parallel rhythmic pattern; the basic reliance upon stringed instruments (the banjo, which enjoyed widespread popularity before the 1890s mass-marketing of the guitar, is of African origin); the role of the blues singer in society (the griot, a kind of epic poet and singer, still occupies a roughly similar position in West Africa); vocal techniques like melisma (the stretching of a single syllable over several notes), falsetto, and the microtonal flattening of third and seventh notes in the scale. Even some of the language has been preserved, with all-purpose words like "dig" and "jive" relating back to the Wolof tribe's "dega" and "jev" and even so common a word as "juke" appearing to derive from the closely related Bambara tribe's "dzugu" (both Wolof and Bambara are from the Senegambian West Coast). The blues is an Afro-*American* invention, however, and the conditions under which black people both came to and lived in this country—that is, slavery and its aftermath—were the primary crucible in which the blues was shaped.

Origins

The blues appears to have derived from three basic inheritances, along with a system of law (slavery and then segregation) that maintained black culture as a separate entity at first formally and then long after the formal conditions of slavery had ceased. To begin with, the blues was preceded by a tradition of work songs encouraged by a plantation system and a pre-industrialized South that not only glorified agrarianism but required the coordinated effort of vast numbers of laborers to survive.

After Emancipation, the group work songs gave way more to individual calls or "field hollers." In both cases, the songs were for the most part slow and rhythmic, suitable accompaniment for the strokes of an axe or the picking of cotton, and employing many of the vocal and melodic techniques—the habit of twisting or worrying a line or stretching out a single syllable over the course of several measures, the disregard for traditional Western melodic resolution, the free use of time signatures along with the retention of an exceptionally strong and rooted rhythmic drive—which were eventually to become commonplace in the blues. The form seems to have derived from a call-and-response pattern in which, in the work song, a single line was stated by the leader and then repeated by the work gang several times, to make up the first in a string of virtually endless "verses." The second "verse," while not necessarily related thematically, would often present a rhyme for the first. In a typical field holler the same pattern might be extended, with a single line repeated three times, followed by a rhyming verse. This call-and-response pattern clearly evolved slowly and was an ingrained part of the Afro-American experience, which remained predominantly rural until the start of the 20th century.

The second major source of the blues was the church, especially church music, despite the fact that blues has often been classified at the other end of the spectrum from gospel songs, regarded as "devil's music," and shunned by former sinners who have officially embraced the faith. Nonetheless, there are many similarities between the two musics, sacred and profane, to the point that Big Bill Broonzy, when speaking of Ray Charles's stylistic amalgamation of the two in the mid-1950s, declared indignantly, "He's mixing the blues with the spirituals. He should be singing in a church."

What the blues derived from spirituals to begin with was feeling—feeling and rhythm—plus the opportunity to express oneself in song, something that was not altogether to be taken for granted in slavery times. Throughout much of the South, in fact, various states' Black Codes prohibited the beating of drums, since "talking drums" were a traditional way for Africans to communicate and slaveowners feared the secret fomenting of revolt. Work songs, of course, were encouraged, and Christianity was seen as a pacifier, a civilizing impulse if you will, of both the heathen strain and the heathen himself. Ironically, the singing of spirituals came to represent something of a vehicle for expressing true feelings, not by double-entendre exactly but certainly by suggestion, as lyrics like "I'm going to sit at the welcome table" symbolized not only wishful thinking but, at least inferentially, equal social treatment here on earth. Most of all, though, spiritual music served as a vehicle for the maintenance and preservation of African polyrhythms, antiphonal singing, and a freedom of musical expression that encouraged vocal virtuosity and eventually led to the cross-pollination of gospel and blues which became contemporary rhythm and blues. At the same time it permitted the cross-pollination of white music with black: much of the body of religious music was derived from conventional hymns and white-authored songs employing European melodic progressions and major chord resolutions that were then altered, sometimes startlingly so, by this African mu-

An important source of the blues was an entertainment tradition that eventually developed into the minstrel show.
Courtesy of *Living Blues*

sic, in the words of one European traveler, so "extraordinarily wild and unaccountable."

The last principal source of the blues was an entertainment tradition that unquestionably grew up with the conditions of slavery but may equally have sprung from African traditions of celebration. On the plantations, slaves were consistently used to provide entertainment, a social convenience springing both from the owners' recognition of the African aptitude for music and the degree to which it was valued within black culture. The slaves did not sing their own songs, though a recital program of spirituals sung in a formal, concert hall manner was not at all uncommon. Instead they sang standard white repertoire, including Schubert lieder, and an array of "coon songs" and "minstrel songs," both sentimental and humorous, designed more or less to bear out, if not parody, the prevailing view of the "grinning darky" (the songs of Stephen Foster might provide the best and most enduring analogue). While it may be difficult to see the direct musical link between these songs and the blues, it is undeniable that they extended and reinforced the role of blacks as entertainers and that they played a part in a very odd historical process as well. For white entertainers by the 1840s donned blackface and took up black minstrelsy, contributing songs like "Jump, Jim Crow" and mimicking the manners and music of blacks, much in the manner of Amos 'n' Andy or of Joel Chandler Harris's sharply observed tales of the brier patch. These new songs in turn passed into and were transmuted by black folklore, providing the basis for success of black vaudevillians like Bert Williams—who performed in blackface—and remaining in the blues and medicine show traditions for over a century through continuing popularity of such black-sung songs as "Can You Blame the Colored Man?" or "Chicken You Can Roost Behind the Moon."

By the 1890s, in any case, the tradition of black professional entertainment was firmly entrenched, not only through the minstrel shows but also through the overwhelming popularity of ragtime, a form of syncopated dance music with undeniable black roots that swept the country much as rock'n'roll would do some sixty years later. Other significant contemporary developments were the formal establishment of segregation in 1896, whch underscored not only the principle of "separate but equal" facilities but the reality of separateness and separate cultures as well. In 1895, the first black Pentecostal sect sprang up, thereby encouraging an uninhibited strain of African music to persist in the form of gospel music. Finally, in the 1890s, jazz was emerging in New Orleans as a kind of instrumentalized blues, before the vocal blues was really born. As blues historian Paul Oliver has written in *The Story of the Blues*: "It was this period of social upheaval which seems to have inspired a revolution in the culture of the American Negro and which gave rise to the gospel song of the sanctified and Pentecostal churches, the piano syncopations of ragtime, the polyphonic collective improvisation of the New Orleans jazz band, and the narrative ballad of the black hero. It was also the period which inspired, from the fusion of a number of elements, both traditional and innovatory, the beginnings of the blues."

W. C. Handy

W.C. Handy first heard what he later recognized as a prototype of the blues in 1892. Handy was a traveling black bandleader, schooled in music and the progressive social teachings of Booker T. Washington. "While sleeping on the cobblestones in St. Louis," Handy wrote in his autobiography, *Father of the Blues*, "I heard shabby guitarists picking out a tune called 'East St. Louis.' It had numerous one-line verses and they would sing it all night.

> I walked all the way from old East St. Louis
> And I didn't have but one po' measly dime.

That one line was an entire stanza."

This form Handy (and later blues historians) subsequently perceived as an early stage in the genesis of the blues. Although the form would eventually evolve into a three-line verse, the lyrics that Handy heard that day would persist with remarkable durability throughout the recorded history of the blues, as would numerous other lyrics collected by folklorists Howard W. Odum and Guy Johnson from 1905 on. In 1903, Handy documented the impression made upon him by a guitarist in Tutwiler, Mississippi, who was playing "the weirdest music I had ever heard. . . . His clothes were rags; his feet peeped out of his shoes. His face had on it some of the sadness of the ages. As he played, he pressed a knife on the strings of the guitar in a manner popularized by Hawaiian guitarists who used steel bars. The effect was unforgettable. His song, too, struck me instantly. 'Goin' where the Southern cross' the Dog. . . .'"

It was not until he saw its commercial potential, however, that he was really sold on the blues. He was playing at a dance in Cleveland, Mississippi, and got a request for "some of 'our native music.'" Baffled, Handy played "an old-time Southern melody, a melody more sophisticated than native." This didn't satisfy the demand, however, and next came a request that a local group play a few songs. Handy and his band welcomed the intermission and observed the entrance of the newcomers, who were "led by a long-legged chocolate boy, and their band consisted of just three pieces, a battered guitar, a mandolin, and a worn-out bass." The music that they played was "one of those over-and-over strains that seem to have no very clear beginning and certainly no ending at all. The strumming attained a disturbing monotony, but on and on it went . . . . I commenced to wonder if anybody besides small town rounders and their running mates would go for it. The answer was not long in coming. A rain of silver dollars began to fall around the outlandish stomping feet. The dancers went wild . . . . There before the boys lay more money than my nine musicians were being paid for the entire engagement. *Then* [italics added] I saw the beauty of primitive music."

Within a few years, by 1912, W.C. Handy had published his first blues (which sparked a national craze) and henceforth his art would admittedly consist as much in varying the "folk strains" which he discovered as in creating a body of work of his own. This was the beginning of the formal commercialization of the blues.

SELECTED RECORDINGS

■ **African Journey: A Search for the Roots of the Blues (Vanguard)**

There are a number of ethnomusicological albums on the Nonesuch and Ethnic Folkways labels documenting contemporary Gambian, Senegalese, and West African music and the griot tradition. This one, I think, is as good as any, and more accessible than most. Put together by Sam Charters in 1975, sixteen years after his first published work on the blues, **African Journey** presents a number of different lyrical and narrative traditions, with accompaniment by drums, flutes, halam (the banjo's direct ancestor), kora, and all kinds of percussion instruments. The music is interesting, much of it is beautiful, and there are numerous and pronounced vocal and rhythmic parallels to the blues—but I think this is of academic interest primarily. On a parenthetical note—the record designed to accompany Paul Oliver's book, *Savannah Syncopators*, and sharing the same title, offers a fascinating mix of African songs and blues material, but though I have seen it listed I have never actually seen or heard the record.

■ **Roots of the Blues (New World)**

An imaginative attempt by pioneering folklorist Alan Lomax to tie together the various loose strands and make the connection between Africa and the blues more explicit. Most interesting is the splicing of a Mississippi field holler and a Senegalese one, which for me is as illuminating as anything in the collection above. There is a good variety of blues, work songs, field hollers, church music and primitive fife-and-drum band music on this single album that makes one appreciate the variety and connectedness of the blues. Ignore the value judgments of the liner notes, which denounce commercialization and the excesses of the present day and get a little silly at times.

■ **Afro-American Spirituals, Work Songs, and Ballads (Library of Congress L3)**

■ **Afro-American Blues and Games Songs (Library of Congress L4)**

■ **Negro Work Songs and Calls (Library of Congress L8)**

■ **Negro Blues and Hollers (Library of Congress L59)**

Part of the Library of Congress's (and the Lomax family's) volumi-nous documentation of Afro-American tradition. There are a good number of field recordings available of the various work song and field holler traditions, but these are certainly among the best and most accessible. Much of the material was recorded at prison farms like Angola and Sugarland, where work song traditions were pre-served intact. **Afro-American Blues and Games Songs** and **Negro Blues and Hollers** document the blues tradition most specifically, with Muddy Waters represented on the first and Mississippi blues singers Son House and Honeyboy Edwards on the second. I don't know how you review a field holler, but these are stirring, startling, and mournful by turns.

—❸—
Recording the Blues

Perhaps not surprisingly, it was not the blues in its raw state —the blues which inspired W.C. Handy—that first found its way onto record. Very likely, that was thought too commonplace; certainly it was thought too vulgar. Instead it was the orchestrated, "composed" blues of W.C. Handy, Perry Bradford, Clarence Williams, and Spencer Williams that was first recorded. And even then not without a fight.

In his autobiography, W.C. Handy described the process of writing "St. Louis Blues," a process which might very well stand for the formalization that took place during the first few years the blues was recorded at all. "While I took the three-line stanza as a model for my lyric, I found its repetition too monotonous. . . . Consequently I adopted the style of making a statement, repeating the statement in the second line, and then telling in the third line why the statement was made. . . . To vary the pattern still further, and to avoid monotony in the music, I used a four-line unit in the next part of the lyric. . . . Here, as in most of my other blues, three distinct musical strains are carried as a means of avoiding the monotony that always resulted in the three-line folk blues."

Obviously, Handy had heard this formula in the course of his wanderings. He didn't invent the A-A-B verse; along with the other blues "composers" he institutionalized it. And oddly enough it was this very process of institutionalization, this mission to clean up the blues and expand its musical horizons, bringing it more in line with conventional musical thinking, that gave the first recorded blues a monotony, a predictability that the metrically unpredictable 13- or 14- or 14½-bar homemade blues had never had and continued to avoid, for the most part, as long as the formal elements of education were lacking.

W.C. Handy published his "Memphis Blues" in 1912, the same year that Hart Wand came out with "Dallas Blues." It was not until 1920, however, that anything remotely resembling a blues was recorded, and then it was not anything as authentic as the "folk airs" of Handy and his Southern cohorts. The record industry was certainly flourishing by 1920, but it was perceived for the most part as a highbrow outlet in which minstrel songs, coon songs, and Ethiopian airs, while certainly recorded by blacks as well as whites, were considered to be low relief from a steady diet of opera, classical, and light-classical music. At this point, the existence of a market for blues, or for hillbilly music for that matter, had not even been dreamt of. It was Perry Bradford, a young black orchestra leader from Atlanta, who persuaded Fred Hager of the Okeh Record Company to record a "contralto" named Mamie Smith doing a song aimed specifically at a black audience.

Mamie Smith's first record was not in fact a blues but a Perry Bradford pop composition entitled "That Thing Called Love," backed with "You Can't Keep a Good Man Down." Its success paved the way for her to return to the recording studio six months later, when she cut "Crazy Blues," a sixteen-bar pop blues by Bradford with accompaniment by jazz musicians Johnny Dunn on cornet and Willie "The Lion" Smith on piano. The record sold 75,000 copies in a month, and—just as with W.C. Handy's earlier revelation—commercial success made believers of the record industry.

Mamie Smith's success also set a pattern. If Okeh could have a hit with a black woman singer performing a composed blues with a jazz group backing her up, then that was what every company would have. In 1921 there were fifty blues and gospel records made. By 1925, 250 were being cut—but virtually none by male singers. Nor were there any by performers—male or female—who sang country blues, accompanying themselves on guitar or playing in the cotton-field style that was prevalent all through the South. There was no doubt about the record industry's commitment. As radio gained in popularity in the 1920s, the sale of "serious" music (operas and symphonies were increasingly being broadcast) radically declined. By 1928, the hillbilly and race record catalogues accounted for nearly 44% of all phonograph sales. By then the recording companies had gone out into the field and recorded many of the great country-blues singers. But before that, they had to overcome their second prejudice: that the blues had to be dressed up to be palatable.

Ma Rainey

"You've always had certain people," country-blues singer Johnny Shines has said, "who've looked down on blues as far as I can remember, the gutbucket blues, the backwoods blues. You have certain people who look down on them, even though they listened to the blues at home—they'd listen to Ma Rainey, Bessie Smith, Mamie Smith, Clara Smith. That was more respectable. . . . Now it's true they were singing the same words—Ma Rainey, Bessie Smith, and them—singing lots of the same lines, but they were singing them differently. They were singing by arrangements, and we were singing by whatever came to us first."

Of all the so-called "classic" blues singers (this is how the women are referred to in blues and jazz history), Ma Rainey, who described the first blues that *she* heard in 1902 as a "strange and poignant" lament, probably came closest to the earthy spirit of the downhome blues. Born Gertrude Pridgett in Columbus, Georgia, in 1886, Ma Rainey billed herself variously as "Madamme" Rainey; the Mother of

907, 8921

the Blues; and, with her husband Will, as Rainey and Rainey, The Assassinators of the Blues. With her expressive, gold-toothed smile, her necklace of twenty-dollar goldpieces, her evident good humor, and her bluntly expressed penchant for young men, she conveyed much of the unrefined spirit of the blues, even when she was backed up on record by such jazz stalwarts as Tommy Ladnier, Buster Bailey, Louis Armstrong, Fletcher Henderson, and Coleman Hawkins, and her songs have a rawness and a loose natural feel that would not be out of place in the most primitive of field recordings. In fact, her records surely exerted a tremendous influence on a generation of country-blues players brought up on her music, a strange case (as indeed is the whole history of the blues) of a hybrid form drawing from a folk source and then, in turn, through live performance and records, forever altering the very folk process from which it drew.

Ma Rainey recorded for only five years (between 1923 and 1928 she recorded nearly 100 songs), but she had been traveling all through the South in tent shows, theaters, and vaudeville-style reviews for nearly twenty years before that. This was the tradition of black professional entertainment, which had sprung up in the wake of minstrelsy, from medicine shows like the Rabbit Foot Minstrels or Silas Green from New Orleans, that were designed primarily to sell tonics and elixirs, to the circuit of black theaters, in Memphis, Atlanta, Dallas, New Orleans, and other cities with a good-sized black population, known as the T.O.B.A. circuit (literally, Theater Owners' Booking Agency, but more commonly translated as Tough On Black Asses). It was in one of these shows that Ma Rainey, the Mother of the Blues, met a young woman destined to become known as the Empress of the Blues, Bessie Smith.

Bessie Smith

Bessie Smith was born in 1898 in Chattanooga, Tennessee, and, like her mentor, herself began recording in 1923. Her music has come to be seen as the pinnacle of the classic blues tradition, a claim that could scarcely be disputed in terms of vocal presence or enduring popularity. Possessed of a majestic and commanding voice, a rhythmic assurance that could thrust the beat forward or keep it on hold, and a sense of stillness that suggested vast reservoirs of feeling, Bessie Smith was a pure blues singer even when performing the novelty and vaudeville numbers that were an integral part of her repertoire. She was imposing, dignified-looking, and statuesque, and became something of a symbol—particularly to white people looking for symbolism—of intense racial pride and harsh racial oppression. She sold millions of records, performed in New York stage shows, made a movie based on W.C. Handy's "St. Louis Blues," and attained a celebrity, if not a sophistication, that could perhaps best be compared to that of Diana Ross in our time. Her photographic portraits by Carl Van Vechten remain almost as striking both in their stillness and their vivacity as her music, and for a good while she was as fashionable a figure in Harlem-hopping white society as Billie Holiday would soon become. Even the virtual cessation of her recording career at the onset of the Depression came to stand as a neat symbol of artistic neglect, for she was rescued from an obscurity that came

By 1928, the hillbilly and race record catalogues accounted for nearly 44% of all record industry sales.
Courtesy of *Living Blues*

while she was still at the height of her powers only by the intervention of legendary producer John Hammond, who cut a number of sides with her and Benny Goodman in 1933. All of this is very much part of her legend, but the legend would mean little if her music didn't stand up as well. Songs like " 'Tain't Nobody's Bizness If I Do," "Empty Bed Blues," "Me and My Gin," "Nobody Knows You When You're Down and Out," have passed beyond the language of the blues into a more universal territory. Like Ma Rainey, she was accompanied almost entirely by jazz combos that featured musicians of the stature of Louis Armstrong, James P. Johnson, and Fletcher Henderson, but it is her voice that reaches out across the passage of time, free of rhythmic or harmonic conventions, set apart from the stiff arrangements with which her songs are often burdened.

Her music was enormously admired in its time, and her success —and Ma Rainey's as well—served as the model for a whole host of women blues singers like Clara Smith, Ida Cox, Ethel Waters, Sippie Wallace, Victoria Spivey, and others too numerous to be named. Women dominated blues recording for a decade, but the historical oddity is that this was a virtual cul-de-sac. Since the 1920s there have been almost no women blues singers in the "classic" mold. For whatever reason, with the advent of the recording of the downhome blues of the gutbucket variety to which Johnny Shines refers, the blues returned to the roots from which it had sprung, while the jazz tradition moved on to embrace more sophisticated stylists like Billie Holiday, Sarah Vaughan, and Ella Fitzgerald. Never again would the blues occupy centerstage to the same degree it did during this first heyday, when the music was regularly referred to not only in the pages of the *Amsterdam News* and the *Pittsburgh Courier* but in *The Bookman* and *Vanity Fair* as well. On the other hand, as the blues went underground once again, it could neither be patronized nor formularized, and perhaps that as much as anything else may account for both its remarkable staying power and a vitality that has persisted to this day.

SELECTED RECORDINGS

I don't know of a good in-print anthology to illustrate the various styles of the classic blues singers. The best would have been **Ma Rainey and the Classic Blues Singers,** a collection which included everything from Mamie Smith's "Crazy Blues" to a selections by Sippie Wallace, Victoria Spivey, Bessie Smith, and Ma Rainey herself. This was intended to accompany Derrick Stewart-Baxter's 1970 book of the same name, but since I have neither seen it nor heard it, and since the similarly broad-based **Women of the Blues** in the RCA Vintage series is long out of print, I'll confine myself to selections by Ma Rainey and Bessie Smith.

Ma Rainey
- **Ma Rainey (Milestone: two-record set)**

Undoubtedly the best overall collection, this offers some of Ma Rainey's better-known numbers, with accompaniment ranging from the jazz clarinet of Buster Bailey to the downhome hokum sound of Tampa Red and Georgia Tom. Other good Ma Rainey sides are available on the Biograph label **(Blues the World Forget, Oh My Babe Blues, Queen of the Blues),** and any would be a good place to start, since the Assassinator of the Blues comes across with a mixture of pathos, tenacity, and brassy good humor, and sound quality is reasonable throughout.

Bessie Smith
- **The World's Greatest Blues Singer (Columbia: two-record set)**
- **Any Woman's Blues (Columbia: two-record set)**
- **Empty Bed Blues, (Columbia: two-record set)**
- **The Empress (Columbia: two-record set)**
- **Nobody's Blues But Mine (Columbia: two-record set)**

The complete output. Because these two-record sets are arranged back to front (in other words, her earliest sides are coupled with her last on the first set, with each subsequent issue working forward and backward toward the middle), it's hard to pick out one as preeminent. As with Ma Rainey, it's the voice that counts here and, of course, the all-star lineups that include Louis Armstrong, Coleman Hawkins, Fletcher Henderson, Joe Smith, and Benny Goodman. There are gems on every record, so it's really of little moment where you start, although I suppose I would pick **The World's Greatest Blues Singer** with classic early sides like "Downhearted Blues" and "Tain't Nobody's Bizness If I Do" and the last bittersweet session back to back.

— 4 —

Blues Like Showers of Rain

It's hard to overestimate the prevalence of the blues in the 1920s and 1930s. Record sales don't really document the extent to which blues was played, sung, and listened to, because record sales—and phonograph sales to a poor rural population—represented only the tip of the iceberg. A company like Victor or Columbia would go into Atlanta, Memphis, St. Louis, advertise its presence by newspaper notices and word of mouth, and be swamped with applications to record. A talent scout like H.C. Speir, who owned a record store in Jackson, Mississippi and was responsible for discovering nearly all the great Delta blues singers whom we know, from Charley Patton to Robert Johnson, simply set up auditions in his shop, and the singers flocked from towns and plantations all through the Delta and hill country. In addition, behind every known singer is a shadowy figure who is said to have taught the younger man his style. And in those shadows stand hundreds more uncelebrated and perhaps unnotable bluesmen who simply came out of a similar school. The blues in its heyday was not so much a musical style as a way of life.

"Knifeblades flashed and crap-tables rolled every night," wrote Johnny Shines of life in the Mississippi Delta then. "Women were for hire . . . for as long as you could keep them. . . . The river was full of song, many of it the same as in the fields. You worked every day and got paid every day. One song I remember went: 'One morning to get up soon/ Then I can lay in bed till noon.' That was wishful thinking." In the logging camps, back in the piney woods, out on the levees, in the honky tonks and barrelhouses that grew up around the work and plantation communities, it was almost as if there sprang up a world set apart, an outlaw community divorced from the respectability of black as well as white society. "What'd all be happening there?" said Big Joe Williams to blues historian Pete Welding. "Well, they'd have fights 'n' cuts 'n' sometimes one of them'd kill somebody and never stop gambling. . . . Every payday I'd be at the Good Road camps . . . from there to the logging camp, a saw-mill, anywhere they having a big time at. . . . All though the Delta, I did the same thing. See, you go in, a good musician, and the boss man gets acquainted with you, and all the peoples, the hands like what you doin' and go tell the boss, 'He really good, we need him out here to play for our barrelhouse.' He say, 'Well, yeah, you just stay here and play. . . .' "

It is not at all surprising, then, that when the record companies finally decided to go out in the field to find blues singers, they found a vast reservoir of untapped talent.

Songsters

The first male country-blues singers to be recorded were Ed Andrews, Daddy Stovepipe, and Papa Charlie Jackson, all of whom came out of the medicine show tradition and all of whom recorded in 1923–1924 for Okeh, Gennett, and Paramount. In the next two or three years a whole generation of bluesmen was uncovered, with Blind Lemon Jefferson, the forerunner of a rich Texas blues tradition and author of more than eighty original songs, perhaps the most widely influential.

Equally significant, however, was the recording of a whole preblues generation of songsters—singers who were recorded because the blues was in vogue but whose repertoire included a wide sampling of dance tunes, spirituals, adaptations of white traditional material, pop numbers, and black narrative ballads. Most of this material found its way onto record by accident (it was mistaken, that is, for popular currency of the day); much of the pre-blues material that was recorded must have sounded archaic even at the time. In the case of rediscovered singers like Mississippi John Hurt or Mance Lipscomb, who played in a sophisticated variety of fingerpicking styles, there is an unmistakable sense of a world in which blues represented only a choice, not the single dominant style of the day. These singers represented not a chronological but a stylistically related generation. Henry Thomas, Leadbelly, Mance Lipscomb, and Mississippi John Hurt were undoubtedly renowned in their own communities as the repositories of a tradition that was not only local but also culturally broader-based in its scope. This reputation would not have rested on their recordings—Lipscomb did not record until he was in his sixties, and Leadbelly's records appealed to a predominantly white audience after his release from prison—but their records preserve something of what their local aura must have been like.

Henry Thomas

Henry Thomas, also known as "Ragtime Texas," was born near Big Sandy, Texas, around 1874, which makes him one of the oldest of all recorded bluesmen. His life, as described by folklorist Mack McCormick, is something of a mystery but appears to have been spent mostly hoboing around the South. He was a classic street singer, with a hoarse, powerful voice and a strident, declamatory style that makes little use of subtle nuance or dramatic inflection. The twenty-three songs he recorded between 1927 and 1929, all in Chicago,not only make up a virtual compendium of the styles prevalent from the turn of the century on, but also offer some of the few instances of the use of reeds, or pan pipes (a flutelike homemade instrument common all through the South) on a commercial blues record. Thomas's guitar playing is crudely strummed, his tempos are rushed, and his lyrics frequently consist of the repetition of one line three or four times, but there is great power and a touching artlessness in his minstrel songs, ragtime numbers, railroad ballads, church and blues songs. For Henry Thomas, as for the other songsters, blues was not necessarily a vehicle of self-expression. It was a shared experience in which his entire repertoire and the body of lyrics that he employed was derived from a common cultural pool. It's hard to pinpoint the importance of a singer like Henry Thomas. Certainly his performances were unvarnished and honest, and his significance as a cultural artifact is clear; but what is it that stands out in his music? Maybe it is just that this is all that has survived; perhaps like a faded photograph that is subjected to the closest scrutiny, his music is invested with a greater significance than it can actually bear. In any case it is always good fun, and one ragtime number, "Honey, Won't You Allow Me One More Chance?" has even become something of a folk standard largely through the interpretation of a very young Bob Dylan.

Leadbelly

Leadbelly is a much more singular figure— and one who is much better known. Born Huddie Ledbetter in 1885, near Caddo Lake on the Texas-Louisiana border, he grew up in Texas and Louisiana as part of a large musical family. Adept at piano, guitar, accordion, harmonica, and mandolin, he entertained at backwoods dances and sookey jumps, lived in Dallas for a while, played with Blind Lemon Jefferson there, and ended up in Shreveport on Fannin Street, a notorious row of sporting and gambling houses that he memorialized in song. What he is most famous for, and what may very well have gained him his nickname, are his extramusical exploits, which landed him first in Huntsville Penitentiary for murder, and later, from 1930–1934, in Angola Prison Farm for attempted murder. It was in Angola that he was discovered by folklorist John Lomax, and it was there that he recorded the first of hundreds of songs recollected from a seemingly endless repertoire of jumps, reels, ballads, love songs, blues, cajun tunes, work songs, spirituals, field hollers, waltzes, and cowboy laments. Leadbelly in fact gained his release from Angola by addressing a sung plea for pardon (it was his second such plea—his first to Governor O.K. Allen had gotten him out of Huntsville). He has been credited with the authorship of such folk standards as "Goodnight, Irene," "The Midnight Special," "Bring Me a Little Water, Sylvie," "Cotton Fields," and "Rock Island Line," but whether he wrote these songs or adapted them from scattered folk sources, there is no dispute about the power of his performances or the fact that he made the songs his own. With his high-pitched driving voice, a ringing, boogie woogie, twelve-string guitar style, his impatient rhythms, and his breathlessly forceful narrative skills, Leadbelly was a unique repository of any number of different traditions. Attempts were made to record him as a commercial blues singer, but they were never successful, perhaps because his uninflected style was a holdover from another generation or maybe simply because the blues was not his single strength. Nonetheless, he became, with

Mance Lipscomb never re-corded until 1960, but could handle a wide variety of material from pop to classic blues.
Courtesy of Chris Strachwitz/
Arhoolie Records

Josh White and Brownie McGhee and Sonny Terry, among the first of the New York-centered black "folksingers," an intimate of Woody Guthrie and Pete Seeger, an inhabitant of suburban Connecticut, a charming figure with snow-white hair who played for children's parties and various leftwing causes until his death in 1949.

Mance Lipscomb

If Leadbelly was far removed from his origins by a latter-day twist of fate, his near-contemporary, Mance Lipscomb, born in Navasota, Texas in 1895, was even further removed both by circumstances and by character. Lipscomb, a proud, upstanding man who was a sharecropper and farmer all his life, never recorded at all until he was discovered in 1960 by folklorists Mack McCormick and Chris Strachwitz. The discovery came about when McCormick and Strachwitz, on a field trip looking for blues singers, kept getting pointed in the direction of Navasota; in Navasota, Strachwitz wrote, they were directed towards "a certain singer and guitarist who played for most of the dances and suppers. . . as well as supplying the music for various social functions around town." Over the course of the next fifteen years, Lipscomb recorded material for eight albums made up of nearly ninety songs in almost every style, and proved to be as remarkable a man as he was a musician. He also popularized the term "songster," a label that was particularly appropriate for a musician who could offer up "Long Way from Tipperary" or "Shine On,Harvest Moon"as easily as he could handle classic blues like"Going Down Slow" and "Rock Me All Night Long" or even songs of local social protest like "Tom Moore's Farm," which was actually picked up on popular record in the late 1940s by another Texas singer, Lightnin' Hopkins. Perhaps not surprisingly, Lipscomb rejected categorization as a blues singer and pointed with pride to his ability to play a wide variety of material in a number of different keys as his mark as an educated musician.

Mississippi John Hurt

Mississippi John Hurt, too, correctly cited versatility rather than originality as his musical contribution. Hailed as a legendary blues-man upon his rediscovery in Avalon, Mississippi in 1963, Hurt in many ways confounded the expectations of his discoverers. Rather than possessing a set repertoire of his own signature tunes in the manner of other rediscovered bluesmen, he turned out to be not a bluesman at all but a songster in the same tradition as Mance Lips-comb. He resembled Lipscomb in other ways as well, sharing the same rural background and innate personal dignity, sticking close to home all his life, still herding cows and making music for his own pleasure and that of his neighbors at the time of his rediscovery. Where he differed from Lipscomb was in his having recorded among the first wave of country bluesmen, in 1928, when he was thirty-four years old. His music also differed slightly from Lipscomb's. Even on his early recordings there was a gentle play-party atmosphere to his ballads, spirituals, blues, and fandangos, set off by a delicate finger-picking style less rhythmically propulsive than Lipscomb's. As Stephen Calt has written: "Hurt represented one of the rare recorded examples of black household music: music performed by an ama-teur with no interest in financial gain. . . . His was music with no con-ventional non-musical gimmicks appended." In fact, Hurt's music, and his whispery bullfrog voice, retain a winsomeness almost foreign to the blues and were almost certainly part of the reason for his enor-mous popularity in folk circles between 1963 and his death in 1966. Hurt was himself bemused by his own popularity; he couldn't under-stand what all the fuss was about. And that, too, was part of his charm, and part of the charm of his music.

These four singers—Hurt, Lipscomb, Leadbelly, and Henry Thomas—represent only a small sampling of the music that was available in the early years of the century. Every town, every region had its own Mississippi John Hurt, its own street singers, its own re-pository of musical styles and local traditions. As you listen to non-commercial field recordings, whether vintage sides from the Library of Congress or material collected by present-day folklorists, you real-ize more and more that the whole thrust of creating a retrospective star system, of assigning myth and weighted value to each per-former, as if eternity were the prize and art the entry fee, is altogether wrong. The blues was a milieu, not an aesthetic theory, a milieu where popularity or accessibility (via phonograph records) deter-mined form, not the other way around. It may well be that popular blues singers like Charley Patton and Blind Lemon Jefferson came as much out of the songster tradition as did Leadbelly or Mance Lips-comb. It seems almost certain, in fact, that a purely emotive singer like Patton would never have emerged so singularly had the songster tradition prevailed. One sees the persistence of this tradition, even in the work of so staunch a bluesman as Big Joe Williams, who has proclaimed "You Are My Sunshine" to be his favorite song and main-tains "She'll Be Coming 'Round the Mountain" in his performing rep-ertoire. The fact is, though, that blues records did sell, and with each successive year the blues tradition was more firmly entrenched. In 1925, 250 individual blues and gospel records were recorded; by

*Mississippi John Hurt,
like Mance Lipscomb,
performed in the
songster tradition,
emphasizing versatility
rather than originality.*
Courtesy of *Sing Out*

1927 the figure had risen to 500. Even more astonishingly the estimated sales of blues and gospel records in 1927 came to ten million,
"a number approximately equal to the black American population
counted by the census takers," as Jeff Titon has pointed out in *Early
Downhome Blues*.

Obviously the trend, and the potential income from recording,
were persuasive, and while there remained holdouts against
modernity like Mance Lipscomb and Mississippi John Hurt, other
representatives of the songster tradition such as Blind Willie McTell,
Frank Stokes, and Jim Jackson steered more and more towards the
blues, whether of their own volition, or with the decided encouragement of the record companies, or both. As the recorded blues grew
more and more popular, the form of the blues became fixed as well,
with a regular twelve-bar pattern and a timed-out metrical scheme
the goal. And it was left to bluesmen like Blind Lemon Jefferson
to create a body of well-made blues, which gained Jefferson in particular a popularity unmatched by any of the early downhome
blues singers.

SELECTED RECORDINGS

Henry Thomas
■ Henry Thomas: "Ragtime Texas" (Herwin: two-record set)

Not only the complete recorded work, this double album comes
equipped with a fascinating 10,000 word essay on Henry Thomas's
life and times by folklorist Mack McCormick. There are blues, pre-
blues, ragtime, narrative ballads, and incidental autobiography—all
presented with uncomplicated enthusiasm and that impatient sense
of rushed time peculiar to the Texas tradition. On many cuts,
Thomas's pan-pipes provide an oddly lyrical, flutelike obbligato to
the roughly strummed guitar. Sound is good, lyrics are included, and
for all its academic justification, this is a highly listenable, *enjoyable*
album.

Leadbelly

■ **Leadbelly: The Library of Congress Recordings (Elektra: three-record set)**

The best over-all selection of Leadbelly's compendious work, and the one place to find the full sweep of his remarkable musical interests all in one package. Here we find folk songs "Green Corn" and "Rock Island Line" next to blues (Blind Lemon Jefferson's "Matchbox," "Alberta"), ballads ("Ella Speed" and "Frankie and Albert") and his successful pleas for pardon to Governors O.K. Allen and Pat Neff. The only thing missing is "The Streets of Laredo," which Leadbelly undoubtedly recorded somewhere. Here he is in good voice throughout, singing in higher-pitched tones and with greater delicacy—if the word "delicacy" can ever be applied to the work of a powerhouse performer like Huddie Ledbetter—than on many of his later recordings. The sound is quite poor in places, but the preservation of Leadbelly's first recorded performances—from his discovery in Angola in 1933 to the 1942 recordings in Washington, D.C.—overrides any auditory inconvenience involved.

■ **Leadbelly (Columbia)**

Leadbelly Sings the Blues. These performances were recorded in 1935 and are every bit as remarkable in their way as the Library of Congress sessions, except that Leadbelly was not exclusively a blues singer and to some extent these sides represented ARC's (Columbia's) attempt to channel a songster in a commercial direction. Nonetheless, there are some wonderful moments here, including a beautiful slide version of "Packin' Truck," a detailed recollection of Blind Lemon Jefferson that turned up in different versions in Leadbelly's repertoire over the years, and several repetitions of the Library of Congress blues material with better fidelity. A nice choice if you want nothing but the blues.

■ **Jerry's Saloon Blues (Flyright)**

A fascinating historical document, once again from Library of Congress recordings, including selections by Leadbelly's eighty-year-old uncle, Bob Ledbetter, and Ledbetter's grandson Noah Moore, recorded in Oil City, outside of Shreveport, in 1940. Ledbetter's cut is a quavery but eloquent version of "Goodnight, Irene," Leadbelly's signature tune that Uncle Bob says he taught his nephew. Moore's numbers are two blues played with a slide that show the surprising influence of Robert Johnson as well as a Leadbelly-influenced eight-bar reel, and "Low Down Worry Blues," a hypnotically extended (nearly twelve minutes) excursion into the common pool of blues verses. This is music that is both conventional and unique, presented with serene indifference to its significance or permanency by semiprofessional "musicianers," one of whom informs us confidentially, "There's two places in Shreveport I don't want my woman to go/ That's down to Jerry's Saloon and the moving picture show."

Mance Lipscomb

■ **Mance Lipscomb Vols. 1-6 (Arhoolie)**

■ **You'll Never Find Another Man Like Mance (Arhoolie)**

The last title says it all. Mance Lipscomb was a remarkable consistent performer, and the standard of musical excellence is high throughout. Every album is a good one, offering variety, entertainment, and a good introduction to Lipscomb's music. My favorite albums remain volumes 1 and 2; along with **You'll Never Find**, a 1964 live album that serves as something of a reprise of some of Mance's best and most familiar titles. What comes across plainly on every record, though, is a sense of Mance, a sense of the tradition (a sense of *all* the traditions), and a sense of the most listenable, charming, danceable music, propelled simply by a man's comfortable-sounding voice and cleanly picked guitar.

Mississippi John Hurt

■ **Mississippi John Hurt—1928 Sessions (Yazoo)**

The original sessions, complete, with thoughtful notes and Yazoo's usual impeccable sound. "Paradoxically," writes Stephen Calt in the liner notes, "his lack of professionalism served to make his guitar playing more intricate than that of most blues singers. It freed him from the ·necessity of thinking in terms of dance tempos and thus playing slowly enough to emphasize the gymnastic character of his accents. He could play with as much speed or subtlety as he was capable of attaining through his fingers alone." This is what he did on record, and this is what we hear on classic ballads like "Frankie," "Stack O'Lee," and "Spike Driver Blues" (Hurt's variation on "John Henry"), on spirituals, ragtime numbers, and straightforward blues. A classic set.

■ **Mississippi John Hurt (Piedmont)**

■ **The Immortal Mississippi John Hurt (Vanguard)**

■ **Mississippi John Hurt: Last Sessions (Vanguard)**

To my mind, the best of Hurt's latter-day recordings, fully the equal of his early work, with fingerpicking as deft and a voice as wispily ingratiating. The Vanguard albums have several nice guitar duets with folk musician Patrick Sky. The Piedmont album, Hurt's first after rediscovery, is my favorite if only for its unselfconscious charm—but then *all* are charming, varied, gentle, accomplished, and anomalous exemplars of a very different blues tradition.

5

Blues Left Texas Loping Like a Mule

Blind Lemon Jefferson first recorded in 1926. From the start he was among the most influential of all the country-blues singers, and in fact the influence of his recordings persists to this day. Obviously he was well known from his travels. Born near Wortham, Texas, in 1897, he is remembered as far east as Virginia and the Carolinas. In the single picture of him that survives he appears well-fed, professorial, and content, with clear, wire-rimmed glasses (though presumably he could not see), a black frock coat, what may well be a painted-on tie and collar, a square puffy face, and a comfortable expanse of stomach. Paramount, his record company, advertised the pathos of his situation. "Can anyone imagine a fate more horrible than to find that one is blind?" asked *The Paramount Book of Blues.* "To realize that the beautiful things one hears about—one will never see? Such was the heart-rending fate of Lemon Jefferson. . . . Then—environment began to play its important part in his destiny. He could hear and he heard the sad-hearted, weary people of his homeland, Dallas—singing weird, sad melodies at their work and play, and unconsciously he began to imitate them—lamenting his fate in song. . . ."

Despite the somewhat bathetic description, Jefferson appears to have been an altogether resourceful individual, forming partnerships from time to time with sighted proteges like Leadbelly and a teen-aged T-Bone Walker, but for the most part getting around Dallas and the surrounding countryside on his own. After he recorded, he got a car and a chauffeur, and he is remembered more as a star by his contemporaries than as a figure of pathos. Sam "Lightnin' " Hopkins first saw him at the Buffalo Association Picnic, a convocation of the General Association of Baptist Churches, in 1920, when Hopkins was eight years old. Sam had a guitar with him, he told blues researcher Samuel Charters, and he started playing along with Lemon's music. When the bluesman picked him out of the crowd and praised his playing, the experience became a memory that stayed with Lightnin' all his life.

Blind Lemon Jefferson recorded more than eighty songs from 1926–1929, when he was found reportedly frozen to death in a

Blind Lemon Jefferson's blues stand out for their careful construction, his thin piercing voice, and the originality of his guitar style.
Courtesy of *Living Blues*

snowstorm in Chicago. While he did record a couple of ragtime numbers, some pre-blues, a number of spirituals, and the well-known hymn "See That My Grave Is Kept Clean," he was best known for his blues, and what stands out in his blues are their well-ordered construction, his thin piercing voice, and a guitar style that served more as a cleanly articulated extension of that voice than as a straightforward accompaniment to it. In this he was the first of the modern bluesmen, much in the manner of T-Bone Walker and B.B. King, each of whom acknowledged his influence and followed in his path.

More than anything else, it was his talent for song construction that made Blind Lemon Jefferson about as up-to-the-minute as any country-blues singer of his day. He had a flair for melody, the ability to meter out his verses, and a seemingly inexhaustible fund of original lyrics that immediately entered into the common language of the blues. Ironically, it is this careful construction that makes his blues somewhat less accessible to us today. They are more regular, more ordered, neater harmonically than the blues of many of his contemporaries; the harmonic progression—like that of the women singers from whom he occasionally takes his inspiration—is almost always the I-IV-V-IV-I of conventional Western expectation. This is not to say that his singing, or his guitar-playing for that matter, is any less "weird" than the nameless Tutwiler bluesman that W.C. Handy encountered or the blind primitive that Paramount advertised, but his chordal resolutions are considerably more predictable than the less "artistic" efforts of Henry Thomas, say, or the more passionate outpourings of the Mississippi blues tradition. One wonders if Blind Lemon in person was not more of a songster, performing numbers from every tradition and providing every kind of entertainment—jokes, toasts, and music for tapdancing—for the crowds that assembled in front of the local feedstore, at schoolhouses, crossroads, country picnics, and Saturday afternoon in the marketplace. Probably he was, and probably his blues were looser, less orderly, more wild and free in person than they come across on record. Nonetheless, even on record they come across with strength and an eerie forcefulness, despite their gentility of structure, despite an imperfect and tinny-sounding recording process, and despite the distance of fifty years.

The effect of Blind Lemon Jefferson's music lingers to this day. Songs like "Black Snake Moan," "Matchbox Blues," and "See That My Grave Is Kept Clean" are permanent fixtures in the blues repertoire. Bluesmen like Johnny Shines and Furry Lewis, otherwise staunchly in the Memphis and Mississippi tradition, have always echoed Jefferson's style in certain numbers. The sprung-rhythm guitar work remains immediately recognizable and gave rise to a whole school of bluesmen who imitated the form, if not the tone, of his idiosyncratic playing.

Lemon's music was echoed in its day by the work of Texas artists like Little Hat Jones and J.T. "Funny Papa" Smith, Alabama-born Ed Bell and Edward Thompson, white hillbilly singer Dick Justice, Mississippi bluesman Isaiah Nettles, and of course the whole extended Texas tradition that stretched down through T-Bone Walker to the enormously influential recordings of Lightnin' Hopkins after World War II and even the rhythm and blues that Duke Records put out in Houston all through the 1950s and 1960s. Blind Lemon Jefferson's music entered into the fabric of it all to one extent or another, but it's difficult to link him to a specific school of singers, perhaps because Lemon was so individual a stylist; and so it might be best simply to cite some of the outstanding Texas bluesmen individually.

Texas Alexander

Alger "Texas" Alexander is one of the few country-blues singers who did not accompany himself on any instrument. An older cousin of Lightnin' Hopkins, very likely a contemporary of Leadbelly, Alexander recorded extensively from 1927–1934, with everyone from Lonnie Johnson to the Mississippi Sheiks to King Oliver and Clarence Williams accompanying him in his own free-flowing adaptations of work songs and field hollers. One of the stylistic traits most often remarked upon in Lemon's music is that it sounded sometimes as if vocalist and guitarist were different entities. In Alexander's case, of course, this was true, and the results were sometimes startling, occasionally even disconcerting. No one ever figured out quite how to accompany the long lines and loosely defined accents of Texas Alexander, though there were a number of fairly successful attempts, particularly by guitarists like Little Hat Jones who were clearly schooled in the Texas idiom. In any case, the grandiose thing about Texas Alexander is his voice, which triumphs over any accompaniment, employing a warm tone, a pronounced vibrato, a full dynamic range, and a swelling sense of melody, together with an eloquent, wordless moan, to recreate the sense of the Texas work and convict songs. Perhaps this is no coincidence, since Texas Alexander appears to have spent a good deal of time in jail.

Blind Willie Johnson

Another tradition, certainly separate from the blues but clearly related to it, was the religious music of Blind Willie Johnson. Johnson, one of the most singular performers ever to record in the blues and gospel tradition, played no secular music, but his slide guitar playing,

his fierce vocals, and his original compositions were enormously influential all through the South. Elements of his repertoire entered the
work of musicians as geographically and stylistically diverse as Son
House, Reverend Gary Davis, Fred McDowell, and even Muddy Waters, and, while he recorded no blues as such, the driving force of his
music, the astonishing virtuosity of his vocal technique, even the
confident narrative skill of his compositions helped shape an entire
generation of blues players. Widely imitated as a guitarist, he is one of
the few bottleneck artists, according to Stephen Calt, "with the ability
to sound three or four distinct melody notes upon striking a string
once, a skill that enhances rhythmic fluidity and reflects uncanny
left-handed strength, accuracy, and agility. His control is all the more
impressive when one considers the fact that he picks as forcefully as
Charley Patton, and approaches the furious tempo of Kokomo
Arnold, two masters of the secular slide guitar."

In addition, Johnson possessed one of the most remarkable
voices, or several of them, ever heard on record. Pleasant enough
sounding in his conventional range, Johnson alternated a deeper
register and a rasping false bass that on first hearing can be taken as
either disturbingly ferocious or almost comic in its effect. It's a little
like listening to the Chicago blues singer Howlin' Wolf with sound effects, and the impression created is altogether startling, whether on
relatively conventional hymns like "God Don't Never Change" or on
preaching showpieces like "If I Had My Way I'd Tear the Building
Down" in which a fierce recitative chant alternates with the onrush of
the chorus that gives the song its title. So forceful was the declara-
tion, in fact, that Johnson is said to have been arrested for inciting a
riot by standing in front of the Customs House in New Orleans and
singing this song. While the story may be apocryphal, the power of
Johnson's music certainly is not. And even if Johnson's style is seen
as an isolated outcropping, this does not make it less compelling.

Texas Traditions

What is more likely is that there was a whole Texas bottleneck
school, that Blind Willie Johnson's music hooks up with Ramblin'
Thomas's, and Thomas's with that of Oscar "Buddy" Woods and the
Black Ace, that Texas in fact did not lack a fully developed tradition so
much as a fully *documented* tradition. That this is so can be seen
from the flourishing of the Texas blues after World War II, when the
new independent record companies recorded bluesmen like
Lightnin' Hopkins, L'il Son Jackson, Frankie Lee Sims, and Smokey
Hogg, all playing in essentially the style that first appeared in the
1920s, only this time with amplification. And then, of course, there
was T-Bone Walker, who was perhaps the single most dominant influence upon postwar guitar playing and who served his original ap-
prenticeship as Blind Lemon Jefferson's lead boy while clearly
coming under the sway of his music. Texas had a rich unrecorded
tradition, then, but—except for the extensively documented piano
stylings of San Antonio, Dallas, and Galveston, which are a whole
other story—it came down in somewhat indirect ways. Not so with
the Mississippi blues, which came down in a direct line of succession from Charley Patton to Muddy Waters and was passed on in

equally straightforward fashion to Eric Clapton, the Rolling Stones, and the world of rock'n'roll.

SELECTED RECORDINGS

ANTHOLOGIES

- **Tex-Arkana-Louisiana Country, 1927–1932 (Yazoo)**
- **Blues from the Western States (Yazoo)**

Both good introductions to a fairly broad range of regional styles, with the second focusing more exclusively on Texas. There are good selections by Blind Lemon Jefferson, Henry Thomas, Texas Alexander, and Ramblin' Thomas, as well as nice surprises by Little Hat Jones and Louisiana bluesmen King Solomon Hill and Rabbit Brown. As on most Yazoo releases, the selection is good, the sound impeccable, and the only fault that could be found from the standpoint of this book is that neither album is concerned purely with documenting the Texas tradition.

- **Texas Country Music Vol. 3 (Roots)**
- **Texas Blues 1927–1952 (Paltram)**

Both are from the Austrian label Roots, and while neither offering has quite the sound fidelity of the Yazoo issues, these albums are nonetheless of great value to students of the Texas tradition. **Texas Blues** offers four strong selections by Texas Alexander and puts them in the context of 1950s performances by Lightnin' Hopkins and Smokey Hogg, as well as slide-guitar pieces by Oscar Woods (represented, too, on Flyright's **Jerry's Saloon Blues**)and the Black Ace. **Texas Country Music** is more of a mish-mash of Texas styles, with piano technique represented by Joe Pullum's classic "Black Gal" and Bernice Edwards's "Ninth Street Stomp," three wonderful numbers by Texas Alexander, a couple by Ramblin' Thomas's brother Jesse, and T-Bone Walker's first recorded number, credited to "Oak Cliff T-Bone" in 1929, when Walker was nineteen years old.

- **Two White Horses Standin' In Line (Flyright)**
- **Jack O' Diamonds (Flyright)**

Library of Congress recordings, made in Texas in 1934 and 1939, and representing a whole well of Texas tradition. Otherwise unknown musicians like Smith Casey, Tricky Sam, and Pete Harris sing a variety of traditional Texas material in styles made better known through the recordings of singers like Leadbelly, Blind Lemon Jefferson, and Mance Lipscomb. There are blues, children's songs, ragtime, and religious numbers, most collected in prison (Pete Harris is the exception) with a far greater amount of accomplished slide guitar than shows up on commercial records of the period. A wonderful glimpse of a rich and archaic tradition, making it even more evident that the commercial record companies only skimmed the surface in the 1920s and 1930s.

INDIVIDUAL PERFORMERS

Blind Lemon Jefferson
- **Blind Lemon Jefferson (Milestone: two-record set)**
- **Blind Lemon Jefferson Vol. 1 (Biograph)**

Milestone's **Blind Lemon Jefferson** is a two-record set that comprises nearly all the well-known cuts by this foremost Texas blues-man. The sound is as good as you can get out of the old Paramount recordings, and the selection affords a good idea of the range of Lemon's style, from original blues to ragtime ("Shuckin' Sugar") to piano-accompanied classic blues to the Texas slide guitar show-piece "Jack O'Diamonds." Listening to Blind Lemon Jefferson for long stretches of time can get a little wearing, and my favorite individual album is the Biograph **Blind Lemon Jefferson**, also offers a good variety of material, including the tapdance piece "Hot Dogs" and the classic "See That My Grave Is Kept Clean."

Blind Willie Johnson
- Blind Willie Johnson (RBF)
- Praise God I'm Satisfied (Yazoo)

Together, these albums present everything you could ever want from Blind Willie Johnson, with one glaring omission. "If I Had My Way I'd Tear the Building Down" appears only on a 1957 Folkways album, also entitled **Blind Willie Johnson**, compiled by RBF programmer Samuel Charters. The Folkways album is more like a documentary, with one side devoted to Charters's search for Johnson (including a long interview with his widow, Angeline) and the other side containing only four cuts by Johnson, of which all but "If I Had My Way" appear on the Yazoo album. This is all great music, art of the highest order, though the Yazoo sound is far superior.

Thomas Shaw
- Born in Texas (Advent)

Born (in Texas) in 1908, Shaw was a contemporary of Blind Willie Johnson and a follower of Blind Lemon Jefferson and Funny Papa Smith. Shaw did not make his recording debut until 1971 when he was discovered living in San Diego, but his initial LP is as good an introduction to the various styles of traditional Texas blues as can be imagined. Shaw is a marvelous singer with lots of vibrato in the old-time country manner; he has a broad repertoire, plays vigorously in slide and fingerpicking styles, and conveys a sense of good-humored *involvement* in songs that range from the topical ("Richard Nixon's Welfare Blues") to the classic ("Old Original Penitentiary Blues"). As with a number of other rediscovered bluesman, it is almost as if his music got caught in a time warp—not that it lost its immediacy for Tom Shaw; it simply seems to have escaped any commercial pressure to evolve when he moved to San Diego in 1934. You could do worse than start here, and then go on to Blind Lemon Jefferson, Blind Willie Johnson, Ramblin' Thomas, and Funny Papa Smith, for an appreciation of the Texas blues.

6

Mississippi Delta Blues

The Mississippi tradition is the blues tradition that we know best for several reasons. One might be the region's proximity to Memphis, a regional recording center. Another, clearly, is the perspicacity of Henry Speir, a white Jackson, Mississippi record store owner who served as a talent scout for Paramount and several other companies and discovered the vast majority of the Mississippi-based country-blues singers who are today recognized as the progenitors of the blues. Another, which is more difficult to explain, is the wealth of the local traditions. Strong, easily distinguishable local styles developed around farm communities like Hollandale, Bentonia, Yazoo City. It was from these traditions that the pervasive style of Chicago blues, and the pervasive style of much of today's blues-influenced rock, ultimately derived, and these traditions remain surprisingly vital today in one guise or another. Muddy Waters was born in Mississippi. So was Howlin' Wolf. Elmore James, Jimmy Reed, John Lee Hooker, B.B. King, Sonny Boy Williamson, even Elvis Presley—all spent their formative years in Tunica, Itta Bena, Tupelo, Clarksdale, Glendora—all in Mississippi.

Nor is it simply a matter of geographical situation. Singers like Bo Diddley and Otis Rush, who grew up in Chicago, bear the unmistakable signs of their Delta roots. Memphis singers like Furry Lewis, Frank Stokes, Robert Wilkins, while more urbane perhaps than if they had remained in Mississippi, show unquestionable stylistic debts. There is, in fact, a clear stylistic progression, from Charley Patton through Howlin' Wolf, Muddy Waters, and Johnny Shines right up to the present day. Son House, Robert Johnson, Elmore James— all are in the same direct line of descent. Through them the blues migrated to Chicago, following the route taken by the tens of thousands of black migrants who left the Delta all through the 1930s and 1940s. And in Chicago, the Mississippi blues found its final flowering with the emergence of the Chicago band style of the 1950s in what turned out to be the last wave of commercial downhome blues recording.

Charley Patton

The so-called Delta style of blues singing and playing originated around Drew, in the heart of the Delta, at about the time that W.C. Handy published his first blues in 1912. It centered on a singer named Charley Patton, born in the late 1880s, who was living on Will Dockery's Plantation between Drew and Boyle at the time. Patton's repertoire encompassed knife pieces, church songs, frailed old-time dance numbers and popular tunes of the day—all sung in a hoarse, impassioned voice not dissimilar to that of one of his students, Howlin' Wolf, who moved to Drew with his family in 1926. Patton was "a mixed-breed fellow," according to Wolf. "He looked kinda like a Puerto Rican. . . . He used to play out on the plantations, at different one's homes out there. They'd give a supper, call it a Saturday night hop or something like that. There weren't no clubs like nowadays. . . he'd be playing here tonight and somewhere else the next night, and so on."

It was a rough-and-tumble life, to be sure, but Charley Patton seems to have been ideally suited to it. Unlike many blues singers, he does not appear to have worked very steadily outside of music, and his powerful rasping voice went along with a real propensity to entertain. Some of his colleagues thought less of him for this. Son House, for example, considered him a kind of clown. He would rap on his guitar and throw it up in the air, his vocal asides have the air of vaudeville commentary, and he was not always scrupulous about the sense of his blues. With his evident ability to make himself heard, his strong danceable rhythms, and his broad range of styles, he was the best kind of entertainer to play at the Saturday night dances and all-day frolics and picnics. He was powerful, extroverted, durable, and compelling and he was immensely popular all through the Delta.

What is perhaps most surprising about Charley Patton is that he got a chance to record as much as he did. Local reputation, of course, meant something. But Jake Martin, Henry Stuckey, Bubba Brown had extensive local reputations, too, and never got to record at all in their youth. Someone like Blind Lemon Jefferson traveled so widely that it was predictable that he would come to the attention of a record company, much as he did in Dallas. But Charley Patton was discovered exclusively through the agency of H.C. Speir. How Patton came to him we don't know, but Skip James described an audition in Speir's Jackson store that drew over one hundred local contestants, with each given a few minutes to sing a verse or two of his number one song. And Speir, with his remarkable eye for talent, could scarcely have overlooked Patton.

The first title that Paramount released, in 1929, was his signature tune, "Pony Blues." Over the next five years Patton recorded nearly seventy titles, including spirituals, ragtime, pre-blues, and more conventionally oriented blues numbers. Mixed in among these are places names, people's names, dates, drinking incidents, all memorialized as part of a sometimes explicit, often confusing autobiographical narrative that is further obscured by Patton's habit of trailing off in the middle of syllables and lines. It is not exactly the work of a conscious auteur, but all in all Charley Patton's records represent the best documentation we have of any first generation blues

Charley Patton had a strong influence on virtually every Delta blues singer, including Robert Johnson, Muddy Waters, and Howlin' Wolf.
Courtesy of *Living Blues*

singer except Blind Lemon Jefferson, and the breadth of Patton's repertoire on record exceeds even that of Jefferson.

His influence was not confined to recording, however, and in one sense, recording was simply an outgrowth of his influence. Long before he started to record, in the decade between 1910 and 1920, he had already exerted a direct impact on most of the originators of the Delta blues style, and in subsequent years he had an equally strong effect on the music of their immediate successors as well. Willie Brown, a native of Clarksdale and one of the most sought-after guitar accompanists in the Delta, moved to Drew around 1910 and learned a great deal of his style from Patton. Tommy Johnson, too, as influential as Patton in his recordings and in his effect on the so-called Jackson school of blues singing, came to Drew in 1912 and again in 1916 as part of a general migration from the Crystal Springs area south of Jackson. Johnson returned to Crystal Springs for good in the early 1920s with his lyrical adaptation of Patton's style, and his first records included snatches from Patton's showpiece, "Hitch Up My Pony, Saddle Up My Black Mare," the first song that Howlin' Wolf ever learned (from Patton, in 1926) on guitar. When Willie Brown moved up to Robinsonville in the late 1920s, he began playing with Son House, a passionate deep-voiced singer who became a keen student of Patton's on Patton's subsequent visits to the area. It was through Patton that House came to record in the first place, after House accompanied Willie Brown to Grafton, Wisconsin for Patton's fourth session for the Paramount Record Company on May 28, 1930.

"We'd all play for the Saturday night balls, Willie and I and Charley," recollected Son House some thirty years later. "Them country balls were rough! They were critical, man! They'd start off good, you know, everybody happy, dancing, and then they'd start to getting louder and louder. The women would be dipping that snuff and swallowing that snuff spit along with that corn whiskey, and they'd start to mixing fast, and oh brother! They'd start something then!"

Son House

Son House had a deeper, more conventionally pleasing voice than Charley Patton. House's songs were more regularly accented and clearly less subject to flights of showmanship, but they were no less powerful or intense; and when Charley Patton died in 1934, it was House who was his principal heir.

Son House was born around 1902 just outside of Clarksdale, Mississippi. He spent a good part of his boyhood in Louisiana, and it wasn't until he came back to Mississippi around 1926 that he really got interested in the blues or even took up guitar. Obviously he learned quickly, first under the influence of local musicians James McCoy and Willie Wilson, then from his association with Patton and Willie Brown. Together with Patton himself, House has been assigned the major share of credit for the development of the emotional Delta blues style. Howlin' Wolf pointed to him as an early influence, and Muddy Waters made clear to writer Paul Oliver just how impressed he was. "Seem like everybody could play some kind of instrument and there were so many fellers playin' in the jooks around Clarksdale I can't remember them all. But the best we had to my ideas was Sonny House. I was really behind Son House all the way." There are similarities to Waters, of course: the heaviness of tone, the dark coloration and rich resonance of voice that House claimed he got from his years as a choir director. What sets him apart from Waters is the degree of emotion, the passionate intensity of even his slightest vocal efforts. Where Muddy Waters can be stolid, even phlegmatic, each song becomes for House an almost transcendent experience.

Robert Johnson

What House is most remembered for now, however—and undoubtedly what captured the imagination of his young audiences when he was rediscovered in 1964—is that he was the teacher of Robert Johnson. This is not strictly true, of course. Just as Charley Patton was only one of a whole variety of sources for Son House's music, House was by no means the sum of Robert Johnson's musical education. But Johnson was undeniably in the direct line of descent from Patton and House to Muddy Waters and Elmore James. And in fact he represented the fruition, the crystallization of an entire tradition.

"We'd all play for the Saturday night balls, and there'd be this little boy standing around. That was Robert Johnson. He blew a harmonica then, and he was pretty good with that, but he wanted to play a guitar. His mother and stepfather didn't like for him to go out to these Saturday night balls because the guys were so rough. But he'd slip away anyway." He'd sit at their feet, by House's account, and play during the breaks. "And such another racket you'd never heard. It'd make the people mad, you know. . . ."

It's hard to reconcile the dates in the various accounts of Johnson's life. By House's chronology he must have met Johnson around 1931, when the "little boy" that he remembers was around nineteen or twenty years old, already married and a widower. His early life was emotionally tangled, and shortly after he met House he left Robinsonville and went deep into the Delta to Hazelhurst, about forty miles south of Jackson, not far from Tommy Johnson's home base of Crystal Springs. For the next year or so he traveled all through the Delta, using Hazelhurst as a base. When he returned, Son House and Willie Brown had a surprise coming. They were playing at a little place east of Robinsonville, in Banks, Mississippi, and let Robert sit in on a bet. "So he sat down there and finally got started. And man! He was so good. When he finished all our mouths were standing open. I said, 'Well, ain't that fast! He's gone now!' "

Many stories have been advanced to account for such proficiency in the blues, and probably all of them have been told about Robert Johnson. As Johnny Shines has said about his own superstitious awe of Howlin' Wolf, "People back then thought about magic and all such things as that. I didn't know it at the time, but Wolf was a tractor driver. As far as I knew, he could have crawled out of a cave, a place of solitude, after a full week's rest, to serenade us. I thought he was a magic man, he looked different than anyone I'd seen, and I come along and say, a guy that played like Wolf, he'd sold his soul to the devil."

Robert Johnson, like Tommy Johnson before him, was said to have met a big black man (the Devil) at a crossroads, had his guitar tuned and then handed back to him. Whatever the prosaic reality, the stories indicate the depth of commitment that came through in both Johnsons' playing and the sense of wonder it aroused in their audience. Almost immediately Robert Johnson acquired a reputation and a legend. One reason for the widespread nature of his influence was that he traveled so much. Unlike Blind Lemon Jefferson and Charley Patton, Johnson never recorded much (his entire recorded output is confined to two Texas sessions in 1936 and 1937; when Vocalion sought him for a third, he was already dead), but he traveled more extensively than either one—according to Johnny Shines all through Texas, Arkansas, Kentucky, Illinois, Indiana, Canada, and New York. In 1938 he was poisoned by a jealous husband, dead at the age of twenty-seven.

There are any number of reasons for the reputation Johnson has achieved since his death. One, of course, is his music, which will very likely endure any changes of fashion or season. Perhaps equally pertinent to contemporary mythology, however, is the fact that Robert Johnson fulfills in every way the requisite qualities of the blues myth. Doomed, haunted, dead at an early age; desperate, driven, a brief flickering of tormented genius.

The songs themselves bear out these romantic associations. "Got to keep moving, got to keep moving, blues falling down like hail/ And the day keep 'minding me/ There's a hellhound on my trail." "I got stones in my passway, and my road seems dark as night." "Me and the devil was walking side by side/ I'm going to beat my woman till I get satisfied." "Early this morning when you knocked upon my door/ I said, Hello, Satan. I believe it's time to go."

In his brief lifetime, Robert Johnson absorbed a good many influences—Lonnie Johnson, the Delta bluesmen, Kokomo Arnold, Leroy Carr and Scrapper Blackwell. What made his work unique was his uncommon ability to synthesize these influences and a poetic sensibility that drew its inspiration from highly disparate sources and transformed them, often with startling originality. Every one of his blues is a carefully worked-out composition, and the lyrics are the highest flowering of the blues language.

His music is more than a match for the words to which it is set. His voice—more accessible in its light, clear, slightly nasal tone than Charley Patton's or that of other Delta bluesmen—possesses a passionate intensity emphasized all the more by its occasionally choked tone. Son House didn't like his voice, apparently because it was not always fully under control, but this, too, was probably calculation as much as pure emotional engagement. Johnson was, according to House, a much better guitarist than singer, and from his records it is evident that he was highly accomplished in a number of styles, including the walking bass (adapted from the piano) that subsequently became a staple of the Chicago blues. The most striking of his styles, however, was the familiar slide technique of the Delta, which he adapted to the nervous rhythms of his music with devastating effect. "This sound affected most women in a way that I could never understand," said Johnny Shines. "I said he had a talking guitar."

That he was a deliberate, highly conscious artist is borne out by the extent and breadth of his original repertoire. It has come down to us over the years in the adaptations by countless singers of such songs as "Dust My Broom," "Sweet Home Chicago," "Walking Blues," "Stop Breaking Down," and "Rambling On My Mind," cornerstones of the Chicago blues style twenty years down the road. His stepson, Robert Jr. Lockwood, as experimental in his own way as Johnson, carried on Johnson's style for years after his death. Muddy Waters's early recordings bore Johnson's stamp on every note. Elmore James, the most intense of contemporary bluesmen, took Johnson's "Dust My Broom" and practically made a career of it. Many other less celebrated bluesmen kept Johnson's music alive, whether or not they were aware of the authorship of the material they were performing. And, of course, Johnny Shines, along with Lockwood Johnson's most devoted disciple and certainly his most frequent traveling companion, has, like Lockwood, extended the tradition with brilliant original compositions and interpretations that capture the fire of Johnson's own performances.

This is the mainstream of the Mississippi blues, as we know it. At least it is what has come down on record and what has survived as art. There were, however, other equally rich traditions that might be seen almost as tributaries along the way. Arthur Crudup, one of the chief influences on the young Elvis Presley and the author of Presley's first recorded song, played with Sonny Boy Williamson, Big Joe Williams, and Elmore James and was a composer of note; but aside from a few distinctive performances he lacked the fire and the instrumental skill to come across as effectively on records as did his cohorts. Tommy McClennan and Robert Petway, natives of the Yazoo City area, approximated the rough-voiced vocal ferocity of Charley Patton, and McClennan in particular recorded a number of highly influential tunes ("Whiskey Headed Woman," "Bottle It Up and Go," "Cross Cut Saw"), but whatever influence they exerted is seen more in each other's work than in any recorded school of singers.

Fred McDowell

Fred McDowell, on the other hand, was a member of an older generation (he was born in 1905) who was not recorded until his discovery by Alan Lomax in Como, Mississippi in 1959. A driving, somewhat unimaginative, but enormously propulsive bottleneck guitarist, he recorded primarily for Chris Strachwitz's specialist label, Arhoolie, from 1964 until his death in 1972. After working as a day laborer all his life and singing at jook joints, country picnics, and house parties, he played for appreciative audiences all over the world, and despite a limited repertoire became an enormously influential figure, not only for other bluesmen like Robert Pete Williams who encountered him at blues and folk festivals but for younger pop stars like Bonnie Raitt and the Rolling Stones as well.

Bukka White and Big Joe Williams

More significant from the standpoint of both influence and artistry are Bukka White (Booker T. Washington White) and Big Joe Williams, two of the most accomplished and idiosyncratic of stylists, both strongly influenced by Charley Patton, both equally adept in standard and bottleneck accompaniment, both equally widely known and yet in many ways without visible musical heirs. White, an uncle of B.B. King, put together one of the most emotionally compelling and moving autobiographical bodies of work, in many ways similar to that of Robert Johnson in its consciously thought-out lyrics, vocal intensity, and taut interplay between voice and guitar. As with Johnson there is a poetic sensibility at work, though the frame of reference and even the craft itself (the rhymes and vocabulary are tightly constricted) are much less expansive than Johnson's.

Big Joe Williams is something of a different case. Born in 1903 in Crawford, outside the Delta, Williams has spent almost his entire life crisscrossing the countryside making his living from music, the virtual definition of the itinerant bluesman. He was widely recorded in the 1930s and 1940s and has continued recording as folk singer, country bluesman, even with a psychedelic Chicago blues band behind him right through the 1970s. Credited with the authorship of one blues standard, "Baby, Please Don't Go," Williams exerted a powerful influence on such singers as Muddy Waters and probably even Robert Johnson, eight years his junior; but his greater significance lies in his own idiosyncratic achievement, his booming voice, his nervous jiggling rhythms (only on the early records; his later recordings are rock-solid), his unique nine-string guitar sound—his very *individuation*. With Bukka White—and Charley Patton, Son House, and Robert Johnson—Big Joe Williams represents the very pinnacle of the blues tradition, even if he does not fit neatly into a historical pigeonhole.

Tommy Johnson

Tommy Johnson is no less significant an artist, although it is easier to point to both his antecedents and his heirs. We know his connections to Charley Patton, how he went to Drew as a young man and came back home to Crystal Springs with a full-fledged style. We can see his visible heirs: the Jackson school of singers that grew up

Skip James, the foremost bluesman of the Bentonia school,
played an idiosyncratic blues that used falsetto singing and D
minor guitar tuning.
Courtesy of David Gahr/*Sing Out*

around him, bluesmen like Shirley Griffith, Roosevelt Holts, Houston
Stackhouse, Floyd Jones, Robert Nighthawk, even Howlin' Wolf,
who preserved not only his delicate filagreed style but his very repertoire as well. Obviously he represents quite a stylistic contrast to Patton, despite their historical link. Quiet, subdued, essentially lyrical,
with a highly developed sense of melody and intricate guitar parts
that vary little from song to song, his music is characteristically punctuated by the wordless and moving falsetto cry that Wolf, whose first
allegiance was to Patton, adopted as his howl. "Canned heat, oh
canned heat, mama/Canned heat is killing me," sings Johnson in
one of his better-known songs, and it is that same sense of wistful
regret that marks all his compositions. Unlike Patton or Blind Lemon
Jefferson or even Robert Johnson, Tommy Johnson recorded very
little for a singer of his eminence. There is no question of his influence, however. Nearly every one of his songs has permanently entered the language of the blues, and, as blues historian David Evans
has written, "For about thirty years Tommy Johnson was perhaps
the most important and influential blues singer in the state of
Mississippi."

Skip James

Finally, there is the oddest, most idiosyncratic, and in many ways
most self-consciously "artistic" movement of all, the so-called Bentonia school of blues players, which originated in Bentonia and
spread as far as Jackson and Yazoo City, centering on a falsetto style
of singing and an open D-minor guitar tuning quite unlike anything
else in the blues. For many years it was thought that Skip James was
the sole representative of this school, that it was not really a school at
all but the *sui generis* work of one man who was recorded through
H.C. Speir's agency in 1931. It was only after James was rediscovered
in 1964 that subsequent field research unearthed a whole school of

musicians who played very much in the same vein. Before his rediscovery, various fanciful explanations were put forward to account for
the eerie quality of the sound. Occidental vocals set against oriental
scales. A unique, specially manufactured, and long since discontin-
ued guitar which alone could produce the hollow doomy tones of the
recordings. An imperfect recording process. None of these explanations, of course, turned out to be true, as James reproduced his music on a perfectly ordinary guitar on an overcast summer's day at the
Newport Folk Festival in 1964. Even more surprisingly, it then turned
out that James had learned to play from Henry Stuckey, a member of
a school of Bentonia musicians who appear to have originated the
style, and that there remained in Bentonia a number of musicians
who shared both style and repertoire. While this discovery created
consternation among some blues historians, it probably should be
taken as one more proof—if further proof were needed—that the
blues is a shared tradition, that it is not originality so much as feeling
that counts, however much histories like this one may seek to link up
the names and point to the progenitors.

SELECTED RECORDINGS

GENERAL ANTHOLOGIES

■ **The Mississippi Blues Vols. I–III (Origin Jazz Library)**

Origin was the first of the specialist record labels to begin, in the
early 1960s, to offer an in-depth look at the various regional styles of
the country blues. Subsequent reissue programs—particularly
Yazoo—have provided better sound, but none has offered better
music. Vol. I is probably the most essential, with seminal sides by
Son House, Skip James, Bukka White, Reverend Robert Wilkins,
and Mississippi John Hurt, along with equally memorable contributions by Willie Brown and the more obscure William Harris and Kid
Bailey. Vols. 2 and 3 continue along the same lines, with numbers
that are more generally available now on other collections or on individual showcase albums. Taken as a whole, though, this series provides an unsurpassed introduction to the Mississippi blues and can
serve as a means of sorting out just which of the Mississippi bluesmen (including Charley Patton, Robert Johnson, and Big Joe Williams) the discriminating listener might want to hear more of.

■ **Mississippi Blues 1927–1941 (Yazoo)**
■ **Mississippi Moaners (Yazoo)**
■ **Lonesome Road Blues (Yazoo)**

Virtually the same things might be said of this series as of the Origin
set above. Yazoo came later, and so missed out on some of the Origin
treasures (the Son House 1930 Paramount recordings in particular).
On the other hand, the sound on the Yazoo records is considerably
improved, preserving a lot more of the highs without increasing distortion, and several of the Origin selections—Skip James in
particular—have been remastered to good effect. There is more
Skip James, more Charley Patton, more Robert Johnson, more
Bukka White. Again, the first volume is the most essential, but it
would be hard to choose between the three on either aesthetic or
historical grounds. **Lonesome Road Blues** extends the territory a lit-

tle with interesting selections by Robert Petway, Mister Freddie Spru-
ell (perhaps the earliest recorded Mississippi Delta bluesman) and
Robert Jr. Lockwood's signature tune, "Take a Little Walk With Me,"
recorded in Chicago in 1941 and representing the first stylistic step
beyond Robert Johnson, from whom the number was adapted.

REGIONAL ANTHOLOGIES

■ **Jackson Blues (Yazoo)**
   This is the place to start for an understanding of the regional style
that Tommy Johnson pioneered, with three rare numbers by Johnson himself, three by his close associate Ishman Bracey, and a number of songs—both originated by Johnson and Johnson-derived—
performed in the unmistakable style by Willie Lofton, the Mississippi
Sheiks, Walter Vincent, and others.

■ **The Legacy of Tommy Johnson (Matchbox)**
   Contemporary field recordings collected by David Evans from students, heirs, and relatives of Johnson, including his brother Mager.
There are great performances by Roosevelt Holts, Arzo Youngblood,
Babe Stovall, and Houston Stackhouse, which, more than simply
providing faithful recreations, extend our understanding of Johnson's style. These include versions of familiar material like "Canned
Heat" and "Maggie Campbell" as well as adaptations of the kind of
material that Johnson played but never recorded, including boogie
numbers, ragtime tunes, and a surprisingly successful version of
Fats Domino's "Don't You Lie To Me." All are true to the curiously lilting, lyric style of Tommy Johnson.

■ **Goin' Up The Country (Rounder)**
   More of David Evans's pioneering field recordings, this time in the
Bentonia style as well as the Tommy Johnson tradition. Nearly all of
the singers listed on the recordings mentioned above are present,
and with comparable performances, but the real surprise here is the
work of Jack Owens and Cornelius Bright, both natives of Bentonia,
who perform "Devil Got My Woman" in entirely different modes from
each other and from Skip James, with Owens throwing in a magnificent driving train blues, as well.

■ **Mississippi River Blues (Flyright)**
   Library of Congress recordings made in Natchez, Mississippi in
1940. This is most notable for presenting us with what the blues un-
adorned sounded like. None of the singers on the album was ever
recorded commercially, and in fact we know almost nothing about a
Natchez "style." Nonetheless these performances—solos, guitar
duets, material both original and familiar—come across as forcefully
and convincingly as anything by the so-called major artists. Lovely
rolling melodies somewhat similar to Tommy Johnson's, but with a
flavor that is unique to bluesmen who obviously had a local reputation but about whom we know next to nothing. An album like this
makes clear what a wealth of material and styles existed just beneath
the surface.

■ **Mississippi Delta Blues Vols. 1 and 2 (Arhoolie)**
   Marvelous field recordings made by George Mitchell in 1967 and
1968 that convey just as strongly as **Mississippi River Blues** a living
sense of history bubbling just beneath the shiny contemporary sur-

face. Singers like Do Boy Diamond and R.L. Burnside play driving, percussive dance music in a modal vein, while downhome legends like Houston Stackhouse and Joe Calicott (whose only two previous recorded sides had been cut in 1930) keep the memory of Tommy Johnson and Frank Stokes alive. There is the primitive African sound of the Como Fife and Drum Band and a Memphis adaptation of Blind Lemon Jefferson's "See that My Grave is Kept Clean" by Furry Lewis. Vol. 1 is more various, while Vol. 2 concentrates almost entirely on R.L. Burnside and Joe Calicott, but both are invaluable in suggesting the indomitable spirit of the Mississippi blues.

INDIVIDUAL PERFORMERS

Charley Patton

■ **Charley Patton: Founder of the Delta Blues (Yazoo, two-record set)**

The definitive selection—a twenty-eight-cut, double album which shows the full breadth of Patton's style (church songs and ballads included), offers detailed musicological notes and a complete set of lyrics. It would be unlikely to imagine getting a fuller picture of a first generation bluesman, in this case one of the most influential of all time.

Son House

■ **Son House: The Legendary 1941-1942 Recordings (Fold Lyric)**

These are the recordings House did for Alan Lomax and the Library of Congress, when Lomax was researching the tradition of Robert Johnson. Includes hollers and one extended piece accompanied by Leroy Williams on harmonica. Majestic vocal and bottleneck performances, slow and stately, and full of the solemnity which House in particular projected. Not much different from his six extant commercial recordings (available on Origin anthologies), except for their somewhat looser structure.

■ **Walking Blues (Flyright)**

Issued in 1979, this includes four previously unknown selections by House from the same 1941 sessions. What makes it different is that on three of these selections—two of which last for more than six and a half minutes apiece—House is backed by a driving little band that includes Leroy Williams on harmonica, Willie Brown on second guitar, and Fiddlin' Joe Martin on mandolin. It's an altogether arresting sound, pounding, relentless, the kind of music which up until the release of this record we could only imagine from contemporary accounts. The album also includes several fine selections by Brown, Williams, and Martin, as well as five unique and idiosyncratic numbers by David "Honeyboy" Edwards, an artist who recorded only sporadically over the next forty years and who sounds here much like a very odd cross between Robert Johnson and Big Joe Williams, his two chief sources of inspiration.

Robert Johnson

■ **Robert Johnson: King of the Delta Blues Singers Vols. I and II (Columbia)**

The one indispensable selection. If you were to have only one record in your blues collection, Vol. I would be it. Together, both albums include all twenty-nine of Johnson's recorded songs and provide a portrait of this most deliberate and poetic of bluesmen. Music, lyrics, and the integration of conscious artistry and raw feeling come together to fashion a unique and incandescent testament.

Johnny Shines
■ Hey Ba-Ba-Re-Bop (Rounder)

Shines more properly belongs in the chapter on Chicago blues, but this solo live recording from 1971 concerts by Johnson's most faithful disciple does more than recapitulate Johnson's songs and Johnson's style. It offers up a set of songs undeniably in the Delta tradition but true as well to the spirit and vigor of the age. Several of Johnson's songs are stunningly recreated, along with fine originals by Shines and adaptations of traditional material that recall Blind Lemon Jefferson, Charley Patton, and Leroy Carr.

Muddy Waters
■ Down on Stovall's Plantation (Testament)

As with Shines's music, most of Waters' work is discussed in the Chicago chapter, but these 1941–42 Library of Congress selections, recorded by Alan Lomax on the same field trip that unearthed Son House, are so indisputably in the Johnson tradition (which Lomax was researching) that they demand inclusion here. Not only does this album offer stunning solo sides; it also features Waters accompanied by a country string band (second guitar, mandolin, and fiddle) that includes Henry "Son" Sims, Charley Patton's old partner, on violin. Great music in its own right, this is also history as it might have been written.

Arthur "Big Boy" Crudup
■ Arthur "Big Boy" Crudup—The Father of Rock'n'Roll (RCA)

Something of a misleading title, since the music doesn't *sound* much like rock'n'roll, but its influence extends directly to Elvis Presley. A bit monotonous, as Crudup was the most rudimentary of self-accompanists, but the songs themselves had an extraordinary impact. Included here are Presley's "That's All Right," the first popular version of "Rock Me Mamma," "My Baby Left Me" and "So Glad You're Mine" (two more songs that Presley recorded), and "Mean Ol' Frisco," one of the blues' most enduring standards. Probably the most enduring performance is Crudup's first, "If I Get Lucky," a high-pitched variant of the well-known "Vicksburg Blues" sung with the free-floating tension of a field holler.

Tommy McClennan
■ Tommy McClennan (French RCA)

As with the Crudup album, it can get a little wearing after a while to hear the same fierce imprecations shouted out at the top of McClennan's leathery lungs, but while his work might be better appreciated in smaller doses, much of the best of it is here, including "I'm a Guitar King," "Travellin' Highway Man," and "New Shake 'Em On Down." Missing are his most familiar titles ("Bottle It Up and Go," "Cross Cut Saw Blues"), which appear on less available and poorer-fidelity Flyright and Roots reissues.

Fred McDowell
■ Fred McDowell, Vols. 1 and 2 (Arhoolie)

Fred McDowell made a great many albums for Arhoolie and other specialist labels, but these are the best. The first record, subtitled

Mississippi Delta Blues, gets down his basic repertoire, the dozen or so songs you were most likely to hear him do in concert, played with typical abandon and shouted out with unmodulated enthusiasm in a strong hollering voice. Vol. 2 is more interesting both because the repertoire is more varied and because McDowell is brought together here with Eli Green, one of his early inspirations and a Delta legend who had never recorded before. Though Green was a little out of practice by 1966 when these recordings were made, his gruff vocals and bottleneck duets with McDowell on the traditional "Brooks Run Into the Ocean" ("Walking Blues") and "Bull Dog Blues" are stirring, funny, and full of life, and the album as a whole makes a perfect introduction to Fred McDowell's world and work.

Bukka White

■ **Parchman Farm (Columbia)**

A fascinating poetic and autobiographical document, this album shares with the work of Robert Johnson (and that of few others) the distinction of aspiring to high art. Songs like "Parchman Farm Blues," "Fixin' To Die," "Strange Place," and the existential "Sleepy Man Blues" ("When a man gets troubled in mind/He feels like sleeping all the time") are unparalleled in the history of the blues. Other songs add further details of White's life and incarceration in Parchman Farm, a state prison. Unquestionably one of the pinnacles of recorded blues.

Big Joe Williams

■ **Big Joe Williams: Early Recordings 1935–1941 (Mamlish)**

With Big Joe Williams, both the volume and the high quality of his work make selection difficult. Seldom has Big Joe made a bad record, although he has recorded constantly for nearly fifty years. This album represents his earliest recorded work, including four sides cut with a self-styled washboard band, several fine duets with Henry Townsend and Robert Nighthawk (with the added accompaniment of Sonny Boy Williamson on the latter), and some of the most eccentric rhythms ever recorded. Great stuff.

■ **Big Joe Williams and Sonny Boy Williamson (Blues Classics)**

More music from a superb harmonica-guitar partnership that helped set the pattern for the Chicago band style—this time accompanied by bass and drums as well, which unfortunately have the effect of drowning out both Williams's guitar and his idiosyncratic rhythms. Still, with the harp taking the lead and Williams's booming vocals,this remains a classic set.

■ **Tough Times (Arhoolie)**
■ **Piney Woods Blues (Delmark)**

The first and best of the albums made since his 1959 "rediscovery" by a new audience. Not that any of his several dozen subsequent albums are bad, but these 1959–60 sessions are as fresh as anything he did in the 1930s or 1940s. The music is more driving, more accessible in a way, but no less his own. **Tough Times** is the more personal album, with several songs that allude to his then-straitened circumstances and a moving recreation of his "President Roosevelt." **Piney Woods Blues,** by contrast, just rocks out, with an important contribution by Joe's cousin, J.D. Short, who breathlessly rushes time on second guitar and harmonica but never beats Joe to the finish.

Tommy Johnson and the Jackson School

■ The Famous 1928 Tommy Johnson-Ishman Bracey Session (Roots)

Here are all of Tommy Johnson's best-known songs, recorded in two sessions in Memphis in 1928. There is simply no improving on Johnson's performances, and Ishman Bracey's seven numbers, recorded on the same two days, extend our appreciation of the classic Jackson style. Like the Patton, House, and Robert Johnson albums, this is indispensable to an understanding of the Delta blues.

Skip James and the Bentonia School

■ The Blues at Newport Part 2 (Vanguard)

Includes four selections by James as well as three by Mississippi John Hurt and one by Reverend Robert Wilkins. This captures the dramatic moment of James's rediscovery when, only two weeks out of the hospital, after some fiddling and tuning up, he instantly summoned up all the eerie atmosphere of his remote 1931 recordings. Even on record, you can still feel the tension in the air, and I don't think any of his subsequent, more technically accomplished sessions ever achieved quite this degree of drama.

■ Skip James/Today! (Vanguard)

■ Devil Got My Woman (Vanguard)

By far the best of his post-rediscovery records. Both are dignified, well-thought-out, and impressive selections of James's most striking songs and compositions. Although he could be a lot more lively in person, these have a lovely stillness to them, a kind of dignity that is only occasionally at odds with the crazy life of his original recordings (his piano playing in particular suffers from this latter-day self-consciousness about making a record). For the time being, these will have to do as the definitive picture of a great artist, particularly since there is no good single album reissue of his early work (Biograph's **Skip James: King of the Delta Blues Singers** is a botched, mislabeled attempt, with poor sound, one suspect track, and several inferior recreations substituted for the originals). Stick to the Vanguard and the Origin and Yazoo anthology reissues of the 1931 recordings.

■ It Must Have Been the Devil: Mississippi Country Blues by Jack Owens and Bud Spires (Testament)

Wonderful alternative versions of the Skip James/Bentonia canon, with familiar songs done up as stomps, two-steps, and buck dances. Spires's astringent, out-of-tune harmonica echoes Owens's powerful vocals and percussive guitar playing. Altogether a delightful and invaluable complement to James's recordings, in what should be the first in a series of volumes to be culled from David Evans's field research.

—7—

Downhome Blues and Goodtime Fun

After the initial success of the blues as a commercial music—it should be evident from the proliferation of Mississippi blues alone—the record companies started beating the bushes for blues talent. Between 1926 and 1930, according to blues historian Jeff Titon, more than 2000 downhome blues records were cut, and initial sales of 10,000 records for a strictly regional hit were by no means uncommon. By 1929, Bessie Smith, once the biggest star of her day and author of perhaps the first blues million-seller, was selling no more than 10,000 records per release; that year, the first record by Barbecue Bob, which was distributed primarily in the Atlanta region and very likely never crossed over even into Mississippi, sold nearly 6000 copies. It was in this way that strong regional styles could continue to develop and find a commercial outlet as well. In this sense, blues, then, was very much the rock'n'roll of its day.

Two of the most strongly developed and attractive regional styles were those of Atlanta and the Piedmont, clearly linked musically as well as by a pattern of black migration that drew inhabitants of the Southeast to Baltimore, the District of Columbia, and New York, rather than Chicago, St. Louis, or the West Coast. While there is no line of succession as clear as the Charley Patton-Son House-Robert Johnson genealogy of the Mississippi blues, in each case there seems to have been a cluster of performers grouped around one or two charismatic figures. Who originated each school remains problematic, just as it is virtually impossible to determine exactly where Charley Patton got his style or how the Bentonia style arose. There were, however, common characteristics and a common feel, gentler and more insinuating, than the more urgent imprecations of the Mississippi blues.

Blind Willie McTell

Atlanta was a magnet, much like Memphis to the west, drawing migrants, black and white, from the country to the city. Many different styles came together in Atlanta—Barbecue Bob and his brother, Charley Hicks (aka Lincoln), played in one fashion, Blind Willie Mc-

Blind Willie McTell, author of "Statesboro Blues," played delicate slide guitar, sang in a nasal voice, and was a brilliant composer.
Courtesy of *Living Blues*

Tell in another, while Buddy Moss, who came strongly under the influence of McTell, started out more in the Piedmont style of Augusta, where he was raised. One of the most immediately apprehensible characteristics of the Atlanta style was the ringing sound of the twelve-string guitar, an instrument otherwise quite rare in the blues with the exception of the music of Leadbelly, Jesse Fuller, and, more recently, Robert Jr. Lockwood. No one seems to know how the twelve-string came into vogue in Atlanta, although Blind Willie McTell, perhaps the best known and certainly the greatest of this school of bluesmen, is said to have first heard it played by Blind Lemon Jefferson in person—not too unlikely a story, points out McTell's biographer David Evans, given Jefferson's association with Leadbelly, although Jefferson himself never recorded on twelve-string.

Whatever the case, McTell played in a unique style, altogether distinct from Leadbelly's crude strumming and churning rhythms, with a delicacy that sometimes seems at odds with his blues heritage. Born in Thompson, Georgia, around the turn of the century, McTell was well educated in blind schools, sang in tentshows all over the South, and confounded blues historians for years because, like Robert Johnson, he did not record under his real name, Eddie McTier, but under a pseudonym untraceable in city directories or death notices. A brilliant composer with a flair for melody and inventive lyrics, McTell showed remarkable resourcefulness as a recording artist: although his records never sold particularly well, he managed to record at least one session a year from 1928 to 1936 and subsequently recorded with some frequency until his death in 1959.

This was no small achievement for someone who probably never sold more than a few thousand copies of a record—and often no more than several hundred—but it pales beside the towering achievement of the work itself. There is a sweetness to McTell's music, a slyness, almost a casual insouciance that would seem like the mark of the slickster if it were not for the aching poignancy of both his vocal and his slide-guitar technique. McTell recorded all kinds of songs—hillbilly, minstrel, ragtime, gospel, ballad, and railroad epics as well as blues; some were touching, some were dirty, and some were just mechanical, but all were put across with a grace and a clarity that were distinctively his own. McTell sang in a nasal, almost "white" tone of voice, his diction was quite good, and at his worst he could be syrupy in the manner of Lonnie Johnson or Tampa Red. At his best he achieved a sense of wistfulness that is present to such a degree in almost no other blues singer and that is perhaps most notable in his masterpiece "Statesboro Blues."

Barbecue Bob

Curley Weaver, Fred McMullen, and Buddy Moss were all associated to some degree with McTell, both on and off record as the raucous Georgia Cottonpickers and Georgia Browns (the group recorded in various permutations), but it was Barbecue Bob, another presumed member of the Georgia Cottonpickers, who exerted the greatest influence—on record, anyway. A little younger than McTell, Robert Hicks got his *nom du disque* from his job as a carhop at a local barbecue. Like McTell he played the twelve-string guitar, often with a slide, but with none of the delicacy or subtle variations that marked McTell's music. Together with his older brother Charlie, who played in much the same style, he recorded several duets as Barbecue Bob and Laughing Charley and between 1927 and 1930 became one of the most popular country bluesmen, cutting over sixty songs, including hits like his original "Barbecue Blues," "Mississippi Heavy Water Blues," "Chocolate to the Bone," and "We Sure Got Hard Times Now." His style was certainly persuasive in small doses, but it's difficult to believe that he would have had the staying power of Blind Willie McTell; he died in any case in 1931, leaving the Atlanta blues to be perpetuated largely through the resourcefulness of McTell himself.

Blind Boy Fuller

Not surprisingly, it was yet another blind man, Blind Boy Fuller, who was the focus for the so-called Piedmont school of blues singing, which was concentrated mainly in the Carolinas, with excursions into Virginia, Maryland, and Delaware. Fuller, whose real name was Fulton Allen, almost certainly did not originate the style, but in fact was an eclectic who drew from phonograph records; from a close acquaintance with the work of Blind Blake—yet another member of that enormously influential first generation of recorded bluesmen who happened to be both itinerant and blind; from the work of Willie Walker, whose two issued sides give evidence of his widespread influence on this whole school of guitarists; and from Blind Gary Davis who, as the Reverend Gary Davis, became world-renowned in folk circles in the 1960s, but as Fuller's playing partner on the streets of Greenville and Durham probably greatly affected the better-known musician's style.

Fuller, born in 1908 in Wadesboro, North Carolina, was undoubtedly aided by two factors in his popular acceptance on record. One was his musical adaptability, which, coupled with an aptitude for the deft fingerpicking style that was in vogue and with a considerable vocal flexibility, allowed him to record every kind of music, from double-entendre party songs to devout hymns to adaptations of popular blues of the day to convincing original material, all without missing a beat. Gary Davis, by contrast, while an unrivaled guitarist, was a far rougher-voiced singer whose recordings may well hold up better as art but never approached Fuller's in terms of popularity. The other factor, at least as important as his talent, was his white discoverer and manager, J.B. Long. Long, like H.C. Speir in Mississippi, was an independent businessman who seems to have had a feeling for the music and to have looked out for the blues singers that he discovered. Long fashioned a "career" for Fuller as successful as any country-blues singer's, with copyrights assigned to Fuller and Long, a number of substantial hits, and frequent enough recording sessions to cut 135 titles (more than any other blues singer discussed up to this point) in the five years before Fuller's death in 1940.

The Piedmont School

It was through Fuller that Sonny Terry, a blind harmonica player from Greensboro, Georgia, recorded for the first time, and for a while Fuller, Blind Gary Davis, and Terry were a team on the streets of Durham and Wadesboro. After Fuller's death from kidney failure in 1940, J.B. Long looked for a replacement, and found one briefly in Brownie McGhee. McGhee, a singer from Knoxville, Tennessee who had been performing in much the same format as Fuller, with harmonica and washboard in addition to his cleanly picked, ragtime-sounding guitar, was billed as Blind Boy Fuller #2, while others, trying to cash in on Fuller's popularity, went under such names as Little Boy Fuller and Blind Boy Fuller's Buddy. Though he was advertised as playing Fuller's own steel National guitar, McGhee proved to be only a facile imitator, unhappy in the role. Then in 1941 Sonny Terry, who had earlier performed at the 1938 Spirituals to Swing Concert at Carnegie Hall (this was the concert that would have introduced Robert Johnson to white audiences had he lived), moved up to New York, where he began playing with Leadbelly and was soon joined by Brownie McGhee. It was then that Terry and McGhee formed the partnership that would endure for forty years. Other Piedmont singers followed the same route of migration, and soon there was a whole New York-based Piedmont school, including McGhee and Terry and Gary Davis. Until the rediscovery of the Mississippi blues singers, this New York group was the basis for much of the folk-blues revival in the late 1950s and 1960s.

There were other equally noteworthy members of the East Coast school, but it was Blind Blake, another mysteriously named itinerant of mysterious origins, who was by far the most influential of all the East Coast guitarists. Blake, about whom almost nothing definite is known, recorded eighty titles in the first wave of blues recording, between 1926 and 1932. Though there is no documented link, it is perfectly clear that Blind Boy Fuller for one listened closely to his work, and Blake's heavily ragtime-influenced records established a dominant trend, much as Blind Lemon Jefferson's had done in deep blues. Blake's influence, like Jefferson's, extended throughout the South because of his records and his extensive travels, but I think it would be fair to say that his impact was most strongly felt on the Piedmont-East Coast stylings, where his light rhythms, clean articulation, and virtuoso instrumental skills were much admired—even by artists as independent as Blind Willie McTell—and his nondescript, somewhat stilted singing voice was nothing like the handicap it would have been in the more emotive Mississippi tradition.

This was goodtime music, and the feeling that came across on record was for the most part quite different from the deep blues of the Mississippi Delta. Not that Blind Boy Fuller wasn't capable of strong emotion in his slow blues, nor is there anything more affecting than the plaintive blues of Blind Willie McTell. The predominant genre of the recorded East Coast blues, however, was goodtime music—fast sprightly tunes, ragtime numbers, party music.

SELECTED RECORDINGS

GEORGIA BLUES
ANTHOLOGIES

- **The Georgia Blues (Yazoo)**
- **The Atlanta Blues (RBF)**
- **Blues from Georgia (Roots)**
- **Atlanta Blues 1933 (JEMF)**
- **Kings of the 12 String (Flyright)**

All of these are highly worthwhile. The Yazoo release offers a wider range of styles than is generally understood in a consideration of Georgia blues—including sides by such marginal Georgians as Blind Blake and Kokomo Arnold (under the pseudonym of Gitfiddle Jim). Nonetheless, this is a superb anthology with wonderful music in a discernible tradition and with unmatched sound. As usual, RBF comes in second best as far as sound goes but, also as usual, Sam Charters (the RBF anthologist) offers an unparalleled selection of music—so take your pick. Barbecue Bob, Peg Leg Howell, and Charlie Lincoln all reappear here, though in somewhat more familiar and perhaps more accessible guise. Similarly, Blind Willie McTell's two numbers are familiar to the aficionado and available in many other collections (McTell is not even present on the Yazoo anthology) but still offer a fine introduction to some of the best and most characteristic sounds of the Atlanta blues. **Blues from Georgia** has strengths and weaknesses along similar lines, with one side made up of eight of Blind Willie McTell's and Peg Leg Howell's best (and most familiar) titles, the other devoted to the Hicks brothers. Sound is somewhere between Yazoo and RBF but closer to the latter. **Kings of the 12 String** is somewhat of a sentimental choice for me, since it provided my first extended glimpse of the Georgia blues tradition. Blind Willie McTell, Barbecue Bob, and Charlie Lincoln all are here, as well as lesser known anomalies like Willie Baker and George Carter, playing in the raucous goodtime style and haunting bottleneck mode that alternately characterized the Atlanta sound. Not all the musicians here are from Georgia, the common denominator being their use of the twelve-string guitar, but this is an album that for me still possesses singular charm. **Atlanta Blues 1933** is an altogether different matter. Scrupulously researched and selected by blues scholar David Evans, it contains previously unissued material from a number of 1933 sessions by Blind Willie McTell, Curley Weaver, Fred McMullen, and Buddy Moss but would be worth purchasing for the accompanying booklet. The centerpiece of this booklet consists of Evans's epic account of Blind Willie McTell's life and of the detective work involved in digging out the facts that had eluded blues researchers for over twenty years. The music is as stirring as the story, and the album is available through the John Edwards Memorial Foundation, at the Folklore and Mythology Centre, UCLA, Los Angeles, California 90024.

INDIVIDUAL PERFORMERS

Blind Willie McTell
- Blind Willie McTell: The Early Years (Yazoo)
- Blind Willie McTell: 1927 – 1935 (Yazoo)
- Blind Willie McTell: 1940 [The Legendary Library of Congress Session] (Melodeon)

All show surprising and surprisingly different sides of McTell, along with Robert Johnson one of the great blues *creators*. **The Early Years** is certainly the most essential, containing the classic blues sides ("Statesboro Blues," "Mama, T'Ain't Long Fo' Day," "Writing Paper Blues") on which his reputation is largely based. There is no more beautiful or listenable blues album around. The second Yazoo record is definitely second choice, though it, too, contains lovely blues sides, several sprightly ragtime numbers, and even a couple of titles that have McTell accompanying vocalist Ruth Day. There is nothing quite of the order of "Statesboro Blues," but this is of a very high standard, indeed. The Library of Congress session is almost as fascinating for its interview as for its song material. It reveals McTell as a person of the keenest (and cagiest) intelligence, possessor of a photographic memory, and a musician who is as much a songster (as surely McTell was, apart from records) as he is a bluesman. None of the material can be strictly labeled blues, and while I find neither the ballads nor the spirituals quite as compelling as McTell's most striking blues, this record suggests a whole new context in which to see McTell and many of his contemporaries.

EAST COAST BLUES
ANTHOLOGIES

- Let's Go Riding (Origin) Jazz Library
- East Coast Blues (Yazoo)
- Guitar Wizards (Yazoo)

All three offer excellent selections of the ragtime-dominated showpiece guitar style of the Southeast. Blind Blake, Willie Walker, William Moore, and Carl Martin are names that recur, but with scarcely any duplications on individual titles. **Let's Go Riding** is the least confined to East Coast geography, with numbers by Mississippi and Arkansas singers as well, but in the same flashy and goodtime style. These are essential albums for any student of the guitar, less so for someone purely interested in the blues.

—— **INDIVIDUAL PERFORMERS** ——

Blind Boy Fuller

- **Blind Boy Fuller With Sonny Terry and Bull City Red (Blues Classics)**

The best selection of Fuller's material, with familiar numbers like "Step It Up and Go" and "I'm a Rattlesnakin' Daddy," jump pieces like "Jitterbug Rag" and "Piccolo Rag," double-entendre specialties, and deep blues. If you want more, you can pick up Yazoo's **Truckin' My Blues Away** but the Blues Classics collection is definitely the place to start.

Reverend Gary Davis

- **Reverend Gary Davis 1935–1949 (Yazoo)**
- **American Street Songs: Pink Anderson and Reverend Gary Davis (Riverside)**

Reverend Gary Davis is often dismissed as merely a virtuoso, a categorization that in other fields would scarcely be pejorative but in blues sometimes suggests a lack of feeling. These recordings will certainly refute that charge. The early recordings on Yazoo are fascinating examples of the East Coast style (and Davis's style) in embryo, providing a good blueprint to much of the ancestry of Blind Boy Fuller's music. The Riverside album, which unfortunately has been unavailable for years, is to my mind the best Reverend Gary Davis that I have heard on record—dramatic, impassioned, involving, with even more remarkable execution than on the earlier sides. Only one side of the album is by Gary Davis; the other side offers an almost equally rich bonus, with Pink Anderson, an East Coast street- and medicine-show singer for over fifty years, displaying a wide range of his tentshow repertoire, from a slide piece like "John Henry" to a left-over remnant of minstrelsy, "Greasy Greens." The Gary Davis recordings date from 1956, the Pink Anderson from 1950, and this is an album that is well worth the search. Reverend Gary Davis's later recordings on Prestige and Fantasy (**Say No to the Devil!** and **Pure Religion**) particularly are worthwhile, if sometimes interchangeable, but see if you can find the Riverside first.

Blind Blake

- **Bootleg Rum Dum Blues (Biograph)**
- **Search Warrant Blues (Biograph)**
- **No Dough Blues (Biograph)**
- **Rope Stretchin' Blues (Biograph)**
- **That Lovin' I Crave (Biograph)**

Once again, the problem is selection. These five albums include almost all of Blind Blake's Paramount recordings. I don't know that one is notably better than another; each gives a good sense of Blake's lightly swinging, raggy, neatly executed style. Start with the first album and see how it strikes your fancy, but each of the records offers a good selection, and it's not as if these were emotive performances depending upon the singer's mood or emotional involvement for their effectiveness as showpieces.

—— 8 ——

Up and Down the Mississippi

Both Memphis and St. Louis, like Atlanta, were crossroads on the migratory route from country to city, from South to North. Like Chicago, both saw their own population increase dramatically between 1910 and 1930, and each served as a kind of chrysalis for the blues style that was taking shape, in Mississippi primarily but also in rural areas all through the Deep South. Whether it was due to the urban environment or, more likely, simply because a number of different styles were thrown together and subjected to cross-cultural influences, the blues was changed as much as the singers themselves by the migratory experience. In Memphis, a distinct tradition was established, a tributary of mainstream Mississippi styles, including slide guitar and many of the characteristic Mississippi touches, but more sophisticated, more impersonal, and sometimes more outgoing. In St. Louis, Mississippi-born singers like Henry Townsend and J.D. Short developed a more subdued, strongly personal style, but far more popular was the piano accompaniment of St. Louis-based bluesmen like Walter Davis, Roosevelt Sykes, and Peetie Wheatstraw, either alone or in combination with the guitar of singers like Kokomo Arnold or Charley Jordan. Both Memphis and St. Louis were flourishing recording centers too, another reason they attracted musicians. In both cities, Robert Johnson and Blind Lemon Jefferson are still remembered for playing house parties, drawing a crowd to a local barbershop, picking up something from their urban counterparts, and giving something back to more schooled musicians like Henry Townsend as well.

Frank Stokes

"Handy Park was situated on the corner of Beale and Hernando Streets," wrote Johnny Shines and John Earl in a portion of Shines's autobiography, *Success Was My Downfall*. "A competitive din of voices rose and mingled in the park. The loudest emanated from preachers raising hellfire, soapbox orators cursing the Depression, and blues singers wailing the blues." When Handy Park was built in

1931, most of the early blues recording in Memphis had already taken place, but the bustling spirit that characterized the park was the same that had always characterized the streets of Memphis, and the blues singers and jug bands who drew a crowd were for the most part the same singers who had earlier found recording contracts. Frank Stokes was one of the stars of the Memphis recording scene, an older man born around the same time as Charley Patton (the mid-1880s), whose repertoire covered the same broad spectrum as Patton's, from pre-blues and blues to vaudeville-based minstrel songs and take-offs on popular songs of the day. Stokes, who sang in a booming vibrato-laden voice, was a blacksmith with extensive medicine-show experience, and his duets with Dan Sain, either under his own name or as the Beale Street Sheiks, set a standard for intricate guitar interplay (actually Stokes set the rhythm, and Sain provided the intricate flatpicked fills) that was pretty well maintained for the next thirty years in the Memphis blues tradition. Between 1927 and 1929 Stokes recorded about three dozen songs, two-thirds of which included Sain as his accompanist, but his influence extended long after his recording days, and he remained an integral part of the Memphis musical scene for another three decades. Aside from the minstrel songs ("Chicken You Can Roost Behind the Moon," "You Shall") and the goodtime feel imparted to nearly all the music, blues or non-blues, Stokes and Sain were most notable for their ability to play with one instrumental voice and for the bubbling, onrushing surge to their rhythms that, on a song like "Downtown Blues," took off with all the infectious energy of the best rock'n'roll.

Furry Lewis and Robert Wilkins

Two other guitar virtuosos and stylistic eclectics were Furry Lewis and Robert Wilkins, both born in the 1890s, both lacking the stentorian vocal powers of someone like Stokes, both masters of virtually every contemporary (and antediluvian) blues style. Lewis, like Stokes, was primarily an entertainer, someone who had played in W.C. Handy's band, worked in the medicine shows, performed with the jug bands, and, through his lyrics if not through his vocal prowess, expressed a slyly extroverted view of life and its many pitfalls. In the two decades after his rediscovery in the late 1950s, Lewis recorded a good number of albums, which extended the slim body of his earlier recorded work and bore out his versatility, instrumental virtuosity, and comic skill. The original 1920s recordings included classic ballads ("John Henry," "Stackerlee," and "Kassie Jones") as well as carefully assembled composite blues that showed off both Furry's dry wit and his brilliant slide guitar and fingerpicking styles.

Robert Wilkins, later to be a little more widely known as the Reverend Robert Wilkins and author of the Rolling Stones's "Prodigal Son," recorded sparsely, showed a thorough absorption of the many different styles prevalent around Memphis, employed complex forms, and didn't have anywhere near the sense of humor that Furry did. Singing in a thin, nasal, somewhat off-putting voice, Wilkins recorded a number of songs pretty much without parallel, more personal than Lewis's (one celebrated a famous Memphis barrelhouse where he played) but certainly no more ebullient.

Memphis Minnie played guitar "like a man," and was one of the few blueswomen to achieve real popularity.
Courtesy of Blues Classics Records

Memphis Minnie

Far more outgoing as an entertainer, and far more popular on record, too, was Memphis Minnie, one of the few country blueswomen to achieve anything like the popularity of the men, described by Big Bill Broonzy as "playing guitar like a man" when she beat him in a blues contest in Chicago in the 1930s. Born Lizzie Douglas in Algiers, Louisiana, in 1897, she grew up in the Memphis area and was known as Kid Douglas until her recording debut in 1929. Her first release, "Bumble Bee," was a big hit, and the model for Muddy Waters's "Honey Bee," and several other records that she made over the years ("Me and My Chauffeur," "Black Rat Swing") became genuine blues standards. Like Frank Stokes, she played for the most part in the company of another guitarist, in her case with Joe McCoy, her second husband, who had come out of the Jackson school of blues singers that surrounded Tommy Johnson. Although she went on to record hundreds of blues in many different styles and was a pioneer both in the prewar and postwar band styles of Chicago, her most lasting contribution was probably made in the intricate two-guitar style of Memphis where she established much of her early repertoire and proved her prowess as both a commanding vocalist and guitarist.

Jug Bands

Perhaps the greatest repository for all the Memphis styles, though, were the jug bands. Something of a bastardized unit, featuring kazoo, jug, and washtub bass, and probably conceived of by the record companies in the first place as a kind of extension of the minstrel show and "coon song" traditions, the jug bands proved to have not only remarkable popularity but remarkable staying power as well. Memphis Minnie had her own jug band for a while; Stokes and Sain played in one too; Jack Kelly had a popular band with shifting personnel; and countless other jug bands appeared on record in the 1920s and 1930s. But the most prominent by far, and the most accomplished as well, were the Memphis Jug Band and Cannon's Jug Stompers.

The Memphis Jug Band was the creation of Will Shade, also known as Son Brimmer, who, impressed with the novelty sounds of

Earl MacDonald's Dixieland Jug Blowers, put together a homegrown version of his own. It included, at various times, Casey Bill Weldon (Memphis Minnie's first husband and later to be a very popular Hawaiian steel guitarist in the 1930s), Furry Lewis, Charlie Burse, and a core of versatile musicians who played guitar, mandolin, harmonica, and jug. The jug, which sounded a bit like a flatulent commentator upon the proceedings, added a sardonic flavor all its own, but what was most notable about both the Memphis Jug Band and Cannon's Jug Stompers (who sprang up in the wake of the earlier group's success) was the way each served to attract some of the best blues talent in the city while at the same time providing a natural forum for minstrel, medicine show, blues, and vaudeville traditions mixed in a with a sprinkling of downhome jazz. The Memphis Jug Band was perhaps stronger in the novelty tradition and in fact maintained its popularity as a performing unit for white social occasions well into the 1950s. Songs like "You May Leave But This Will Bring You Back" and "Feed Your Friend with a Long Handled Spoon" maintained that side of the black musical experience and offered a sprightly antidote to the tradition of hard blues.

Cannon's Jug Stompers, on the other hand, brought together a smaller, more compact, more blues-oriented unit. Formed by Gus Cannon, a native of Red Banks, Mississippi, who was born in 1883 and traveled with the medicine shows from 1914 on, the Jug Stompers featured Cannon on banjo and jug, along with one of the most inventive and influential early blues soloists, Ripley, Tennessee resident Noah Lewis, on harmonica. Cannon, who is still alive and who performed well into his nineties, enjoyed belated recognition with the 1960s success of "Walk Right In," originally a Jug Stompers recording, and is justly renowned for such equally uproarious offerings as "Mule Get Up in the Alley" and "Pig Ankle Strut." More significant, though, were the wistful "Minglewood Blues," "Viola Lee Blues," or the inventively structured "Going to Germany," sung as often as not by Noah Lewis or one of the other band members but occasionally in Cannon's own boomingly strangled, syllable-mangling voice. The original compositions are still bright and unfaded, all of the arrangements are carefully worked out and tightly structured, and one can only regret that Cannon didn't get another chance to record commercially after 1930, for obviously only a tiny portion of his repertoire was ever captured on wax.

Sleepy John Estes

Another outgrowth of the Ripley school, and a highly individuated one at that, was the music of Sleepy John Estes, a native of Ripley but long-time resident of Brownsville, who recorded with various other Ripley-Brownsville natives, including Hammie Nixon, the harmonica player who served as a kind of bridge between Noah Lewis and the enormously popular Sonny Boy Williamson from nearby Jackson. With much the same instrumentation as the jug bands, Estes created an intensely personal style with high crying vocals and a body of autobiographical songs that chronicled both his Brownsvi le home and his own experiences. Songs like "Need More Blues," "Floating Bridge" (about his own near-drowning), "Lawyer Clark," and "Working Man Blues" were highly specific in their social and personal concerns, while Estes's versions of "Someday Baby" and "Drop Down Mama" became much-imitated standards. Like Bukka White, Estes has often been cited as the last of the pure country bluesmen recording in truly idiosyncratic style. This is obviously a questionable, if not invidious, distinction, but Estes and White did have some of the last extensive country-blues sessions before World War II. Estes's rediscovery—he was still in Brownsville in 1961—triggered the great wave of country-blues rediscoveries as well as a vital new career for himself.

St. Louis Blues

St. Louis was the source of another, distinctively different tradition. Like Memphis, it served as·a kind of destination for some and stopover for many other migrant bluesmen. St. Louis was a focus for the record companies, too, with Roosevelt Sykes, Big Joe Williams, and Charley Jordan acting as talent scouts and Jesse Johnson's Deluxe Music Shop serving as a locus for blues talent in the city.

St. Louis was different from Memphis in several ways, however. Unlike Memphis, it aspired to urbanity and might even have considered itself civilized, while Memphis to this day prides itself on both its eccentricity, its former reputation as Murder Capital of the World, and its unmistakable barbaric yawp. St. Louis blues were both more and less sophisticated at the same time. More sophisticated, in the continued presence of classic blues singers like Edith and Mary Johnson as well as hugely popular blues "stars" of the day like Peetie Wheatstraw, Roosevelt Sykes, and of course Lonnie Johnson. They were less sophisticated in their preservation of the most primitive Mississippi traditions, and there was less of the easy-going *swing* of the Memphis blues in this retention of a droning, almost modal approach. This side of St. Louis blues has often been characterized as "taut"—and it does indeed suggest some of the intensity of the Mississippi tradition—but dour might be a more appropriate word for the blues of Henry Spaulding, Henry Townsend, J.D. "Jelly Jaw" Short, and a number of others, all of whom came out of Mississippi in the first place.

Altogether different were the piano-guitar duets pioneered by combinations like Charley Jordan and Peetie Wheatstraw, Roosevelt Sykes or Walter Davis with any number of partners (including J.D. Short and Henry Townsend in somewhat more outgoing guise), or, as St. Louis-phile Don Kent writes, Lonnie Johnson "with anybody." These duets and more sophisticated stylings were obviously modeled on the enormous popular success of Leroy Carr and Scrapper Blackwell or Tampa Red and Georgia Tom, but the St. Louis blues had various flavors all its own. Roosevelt Sykes continued the barrelhouse tradition of Ernest "Forty-Four" Johnson, but in an urban context of nightclubs, piano-guitar stylings, and more sophisticated musical tastes. Walter Davis, by contrast, played in a lean, spare style that in some ways had its analogue in the guitar of Henry Townsend but remained unique in blues piano. By far the most influential of the St. Louis-based pianists was Peetie Wheatstraw, better known as the Devil's Son-in-Law, the High Sheriff of Hell, who apparently was born in Louisville, under the humbler name of William Bunch. Equally adept on piano or guitar, he recorded with Charley Jordan, Lonnie Johnson, Casey Bill Weldon, and, in the most durable relationship of all, with the great Georgia-born Hawaiian slide guitarist Kokomo Arnold. While some of the partnerships may have been products of the recording studio, it is obvious that Wheatstraw was the most congenial of accompanists, and as a singer his lazy rolling style, punctuated by the kind of falsetto breaks that were later adopted by both Robert Johnson and Wheatstraw's sometime partner Big Joe Williams, made him as popular in the 1930s—and as accessible to a wide audience—as Jimmy Reed would be in the 1950s. For all of Peetie Wheatstraw's popularity, though, and the 150 sides he recorded, it was Lonnie Johnson who was by far the most popular of the St. Louis blues singers and, with Indianapolis cosmopolites Leroy Carr and Scrapper Blackwell, served as a kind of prophet of the new blues age.

SELECTED RECORDINGS

MEMPHIS BLUES
ANTHOLOGIES

- **Frank Stokes Dream (Yazoo)**
- **Memphis Jamboree (Yazoo)**
- **The Blues in Memphis (Origin Jazz Library)**

Frank Stokes Dream is indispensable, with some of the best work of Stokes, Furry Lewis, and Memphis Minnie. Sound, as usual with Yazoo, is irreproachable, but it's really the selection that can't be beat. **Memphis Jamboree** is a little bit more of a second-line choice, but only slightly, as it does include more titles by Furry and Memphis Minnie, the wonderful "Jim Jackson's Jamboree" with a guest turn by Tampa Red and his Golden Guitar, and great items like Gus Cannon's "Can You Blame the Colored Man?" **The Blues In Memphis** falls somewhere in between the two Yazoo releases. Once again we meet up with Stokes, Furry Lewis, Memphis Minnie, and Cannon's Jug Stompers, with a couple of classic sides by Sleepy John Estes thrown in for good measure. This is all bright, entertaining, instantly accessible music, and it would be impossible to go wrong with any of these three collections.

INDIVIDUAL ARTISTS

Frank Stokes
- **Frank Stokes: Creator of the Memphis Blues (Yazoo)**

There aren't enough good things that can be said about this album. It's fun, it's infectious, it rocks like crazy, and it's real blues. How much more of a recommendation is it possible to give? Whether Stokes was creator or precursor of the Memphis blues, all the various traditions are here, and strongly represented.

Furry Lewis
- **Furry Lewis: In His Prime (Yazoo)**

Almost as much fun as the Frank Stokes album. Sly, witty compositions, carefully worked out accompaniments whether slide or fingerpicking, beautifully realized performances on fourteen of his original twenty-three sides, including two previously unissued alternate takes. Furry's voice is nowhere near as strong as Stokes's, and his rhythms are more subtle by and large, but he comes across with a certain inimitable charm because of the strength of his writing and playing.

■ **Shake 'Em On Down (Fantasy: two-record set)**

The best of Furry's post-rediscovery records, this double album is made up of sides recorded by Samuel Charters and originally issued as **Done Changed My Mind** and **Back On My Feet Again** on Prestige Bluesville. To my taste, these are very nearly as good as the originals, with Furry definitely engaged (he had not at this point made a dozen different albums all featuring more or less the same songs), a wonderful range of material, and plenty of room to stretch out. Furry's voice is much the same as on his original sides, his guitar playing is nearly as deft, and the pronounced echo of the Sun studio in which the session was recorded only enhances the overall effect. "I'm gonna tell you something, and I hope it's not a sin," declares Furry, perhaps with some disingenuousness, "My shoes done got pinched, and I'm back on my feet again."

Robert Wilkins

■ **Robert Wilkins: The Original Rolling Stone (Herwin)**

All but three Vocalion sides from Wilkins's entire commercial recording output. Wilkins is not as accessible as either Frank Stokes or Furry Lewis. He sings in a thin, pinched, nasal style; his songs, while often highly original and instructive in their text, simply do not have the broad appeal of Stokes's or Lewis's. Nonetheless, this is an album that I would put only slightly below the other two, both for its originality and for its variety in offering glimpses of blues, pre-blues, modal, and ragtime traditions. The sound here is much better than on previous selected Wilkins reissues, and though the persona is not as attractive as that of other Memphis figures you get a very strong sense of the man and the music.

Memphis Minnie

■ **Memphis Minnie Vols. 1 and 2 (Blues Classics)**

The first emphasizes the commercial side of Memphis Minnie's recordings, with cuts like "Me and My Chauffeur," "Joe Louis Strut," and "Black Rat Swing," occasionally to small band accompaniment. Vol. 2 is the record to get, featuring guitar duets with her husband, Kansas Joe McCoy, in the great Memphis rocking tradition. Here you have Memphis Minnie at her best, wailing the blues on "Crazy Crying Blues" and "Memphis Minnie-Jitis Blues," offering up sprightly dance numbers on "Picking the Blues" and "Plymouth Rock Blues," and in general simply providing the best of entertainment.

Memphis Jug Band

■ **Memphis Jug Band (Yazoo: two record set)**

"Wonderful" is the adjective that keeps recurring when I speak of the Memphis blues. This two-record set really *is* a wonderful selection of some of the best of the Memphis Jug Band sides. The Memphis blues may not be as hard or as deep as its Mississippi counterpart, but there is certainly no doubt about its accessibility. Here we have every kind of blues, pre-blues, ragtime and vaudeville traditions—well, maybe not pre-blues—with titles like "Lindberg Hop," "Beale Street Mess Around," and "Cocaine Habit Blues," various vocalists and shifting personnel, and a spirit of ribald, uninhibited, uproarious fun prevailing. Not to everyone's blues taste, because this is not, strictly speaking, blues at all—at least not predominantly—but the links are there and clearly visible.

Cannon's Jug Stompers
■ Cannon's Jug Stompers (Herwin)

The complete output of Cannon *and* his Jug Stompers both. The same comments as above apply, only more so. There's a lot more blues here, not only in the compositions themselves (which are interlaced, like the Memphis Jug Band's, with a lot of novelty material), but in the *sound* of the band, the sound of the vocals, and especially the sound of Noah Lewis's harmonica. Notes are by Bengt Olsson, an indefatigable chronicler of the Memphis scene, in his best Swedish hipster style. Nice illustrations, copious documentation, good sound, and good fun. I feel as if I'm repeating myself, but these are the facts!

Sleepy John Estes
■ Sleepy John Estes, 1929–1940 (RBF)
■ The Blues of Sleepy John Estes Vols. 1 and 2 (Swaggie)

The first is one of the two dozen albums that should make up the core of any blues collection. Like the records of Robert Johnson and Bukka White, this presents a corpus of work that clearly tells a story, both personal and universal. The sound quality could certainly be improved, but the songs, ranging from Estes's earliest RCA session to his last ones for Decca, could not. The Swaggie albums give us his entire Decca recording output, from 1934 to 1940. Here, the sound is exemplary, since the tape transfer has been made from the Decca masters themselves; the music is superb; and the only problem is the availability of the Australian Swaggie label. If you can find these albums, they give the complete autiobiographical record. And some of the RCA material (the more jug band-sounding stuff, with Jab Jones on piano and Yank Rachel on mandolin) could be filled in with **Kings of Memphis Town** (Roots), which also offers a half dozen sides by Furry Lewis (unfortunately already available on Lewis's Yazoo album) and a couple each by Robert Wilkins and Frank Stokes.

■ The Legend of Sleepy John Estes (Delmark)

The first album recorded by Estes after redicovery in 1961—and, not surprisingly, the best. The high crying voice is the same, Hammie Nixon accompanies him even more sensitively on harmonica (their partnership had had another twenty years to develop), and the addition of "Knocky" Parker on piano and Ed Wilkinson on bass proved an inspired one. The material is made up of Estes's classic compositions with the addition of a couple of more recent songs, including "Rats in My Kitchen" and "I'd Been Well Warned," a mournful account of his own blindness.

— ST. LOUIS BLUES —
— ANTHOLOGIES —

- ■ St. Louis Town (Yazoo)
- ■ St. Louis Blues: The Depression (Yazoo)
- ■ Good Time Blues (Mamlish)
- ■ Hard Time Blues (Mamlish)

■ The Blues in St. Louis (Origin Jazz Library)

To me these albums are pretty much interchangeable. **St. Louis Town** (the first serious St. Louis reissue) may seem a little more familiar, with such titles as Henry Spaulding's "Cairo Blues," Charley Jordan's "Spoonful" and "Keep It Clean," and classic sides by Hi Henry Brown and J.D. Short, but each of the records presents a good selection of material from pretty much the same artists: Henry Townsend, Peetie Wheatstraw, Jordan, Short, and various St. Louis pianists like Walter Davis and Roosevelt Sykes. The Yazoo albums concentrate more on the guitar sound—and the guitar sound of Mississippi; **Good Time Blues** features a couple of women singers and more urban piano-guitar duets; **Hard Times Blues** offers much of the same mix, but with a grimmer theme and two very eccentric sides by Lane Hardin, who sounds as if he might be playing a Mississippi sitar. The Origin album is simply a good anthology, again with more of an emphasis on piano and less on country blues than the Yazoo albums. So if you want to stick with country blues more or less, go with the Yazoo, but any of these albums gives a good sense of what the St. Louis blues was all about.

INDIVIDUAL ARTISTS

Kokomo Arnold and Peetie Wheatstraw
■ Kokomo Arnold and Peetie Wheatstraw (Blues Classics)

One side contains some of Arnold's best and most familiar titles, including "Milk Cow Blues" and "Old Original Kokomo Blues," the two sides of his first and best-selling record, which provided inspiration to everyone from Robert Johnson to Bob Wills and Elvis Presley. Arnold's unique slide guitar and humming accompaniment to his instrumental solos are very much in evidence throughout, and if this should serve to pique your interest, there's lots more Kokomo Arnold available, though none better. There *could* be a better selection made from Peetie Wheatstraw's more than 150 recordings, but—again—these eight sides offer a convenient jumping-off place, with a number of characteristic cuts (though none of guitar) and an unmistakable sense of Wheatstraw's striking style.

— 9 —

Blues Stars: Lonnie Johnson and Leroy Carr

Of all the first-generation blues singers, Lonnie Johnson probably had the longest career, starting out in 1925 and finding himself caught up in the blues revival of the 1960s, recording prolifically all along. Born in New Orleans in 1889, he came from an exceptionally versatile musical family (mother, father, and eleven brothers and sisters all played various instruments) and played banjo, violin, and piano as well as guitar. In the early 1920s he was part of a traveling vaudeville troupe that played for the Queen of England. He won a recording contract with Okeh by winning a talent contest run by Jesse Johnson in St. Louis.

His blues credentials are in impeccable order, then, but while he remains among the most influential blues stylists in the short history of the recorded blues, in some ways he does not conform at all to our image of the blues singer, either in appearance or in sound. Polished, urbane, singing in a smooth, velvety, almost languid style, Johnson does not come across today with anything like the urgency or the *primitivism* that we associate with the blues. Although his lyrics are frequently inventive and always well thought out, their very construction and careful planning—not to mention a decided streak of didacticism and sentimentality—rob them of some of the spontaneity, some of the intensity that we have come to expect of the blues. His guitar playing is fluid and swinging and full of melodic invention—not surprising in a frequent accompanist to Louis Armstrong and Duke Ellington—but at the same time it sounds to contemporary ears more like jazz or pop music than hard blues. But even if his work does not altogether stand up to contemporary taste—and in some ways, listening to Lonnie Johnson is like adjusting to the polite conventions of any age, like learning to overlook the stilted mannerisms of the silent movie stars who were his contemporaries—his influence cannot be overstated.

First of all, it must be understood that Lonnie Johnson represented a whole new order in the country blues. Certainly someone like Blind Lemon Jefferson was hugely popular—and popular on a national basis—but it was as the representative of a distinctly re-

Lonnie Johnson was the first bluesman to create a truly national style, as well as originating the modern hornlike guitar technique.
Courtesy of *Sing Out*

gional style. Johnson, though he was obviously a force to be reckoned with in St. Louis, crossed all regional boundaries. The style that he developed was no less an influence on Robert Johnson in Mississippi than it was on T-Bone Walker in Texas, and in some ways it was no less easily assimilated back into the newly transformed regional style. He was the beginning, in other words, of a truly national blues style, long before the blues were ever widely played on the radio (the Grand Ole Opry, by contrast, was started in 1925). His achievement can be seen as the undoing of the parochial approach, and yet clearly Robert Johnson pays stylistic tribute to him in one of his most idiosyncratic masterpieces, "Me and the Devil," which takes off brilliantly from Lonnie's own "Blue Ghost Blues."

His other great contribution, of course, was his guitar style. Lonnie Johnson was the first great modern blues guitarist, the first to make a clean break with the strummed pre-blues styles of the past, the first to initiate the single-string, hornlike style that would soon become the standard for jazz and blues and would provide a direct model for T-Bone Walker and B.B. King, the progenitors of a whole new (if old) postwar sound. Perhaps because of Johnson's musical sophistication, perhaps because of his habit of taking short solo breaks in a jazz context, Johnson's early blues solos sometimes sound overly prepared, lack the warmth and seeming spontaneity of T-Bone Walker's jump sides (but then, Walker's were with a band). Nonetheless, his clear, ringing tone, his melodic invention, his separation of instrumental and vocal lines so that the instrument became more of an extension of the vocal than a rough accompaniment to it, above all his lightly swinging style and determinedly modernistic approach all had an enormous impact at the time and remain objects of admiration, if not of fanatic devotion, to this day.

Leroy Carr

Leroy Carr had much the same kind of impact and popularity, and when he died in 1935, the reaction in the black community was one of national mourning: a spate of recordings by artists like Leroy's

Scrapper Blackwell (on guitar) and Leroy Carr (on piano) had an inspired partnership that produced a long string of blues standards.
Courtesy of *Living Blues*

Buddy that paid tribute to a fallen comrade. Like Johnson, Carr had an easy-going, almost soothing vocal style, sang carefully composed songs that reflected universal more than personal or strictly local themes, and played the piano in a manner that suggested greater sophistication than the two-fisted approach of the great barrelhouse pianists. Where Carr differed from Johnson was in his lack of any real instrumental virtuosity (though here, too, there were parallels, for while Carr's piano playing was conventional enough, his guitar-playing partner, Scrapper Blackwell, provided impeccably crafted, Lonnie Johnson-influenced, single-string fills) and in his continued accessibility to today's musical tastes. For though his blues were far more regular, both lyrically and metrically, than the rough-edged country blues of Mississippi or even the well-rehearsed blues of Memphis, nonetheless Carr's warm insinuating voice possessed a kind of mellow urbanity, a streetcorner authenticity that remains convincing today.

Born in Nashville in 1905, Carr came to Indianapolis at an early age and was teamed up with Blackwell for recording purposes by an English record store owner named Guernsey. It was an inspired partnership, and they hit with what may have been the rural blues' first million-seller on their first time out together, when they cut "How Long How Long Blues" in June of 1928. Over the next seven years Carr and an Indianapolis schoolteacher named Flossie Franklin carefully fashioned a succession of blues on traditional themes which rapidly became standards and have remained so for over fifty years. "Prison Bound," "How Long," "Mean Mistreater Mama," "Blues Before Sunrise," all show up in the repertoire of countless contemporary blues singers and were enormously influential on the writing and musical thinking of such contemporary figures as Robert Johnson and Big Bill Broonzy. In fact, it could be said that one of the things Johnson was trying to do with his music was to combine the guitar sophistication of Scrapper Blackwell and the walking bass of Carr's piano. All you have to do is listen to Carr's "Blues Before Sunrise" and Johnson's "Kind Hearted Woman" to know where much of Johnson's inspiration came from, and many of Broonzy's most familiar hits may well owe their genesis to Carr's and Blackwell's model.

There is no doubt about the significance of the music of Lonnie Johnson and Leroy Carr, but almost equally significant was its effect. With the success of such stable and urbane "stars," there was no longer much need for the record companies to go out on expensive, inconvenient, and time-consuming trips into the field. From the onset of the Depression, then, the companies pretty much stuck to talent already discovered or allowed the talent to come to them, as blues became no longer a folk music but a centralized business, much as rock 'n' roll would become a quarter of a century later. The biggest of the recording centers in the new scheme of things was Chicago, and Chicago was home base for the most influential blues styles from the 1930s on.

SELECTED RECORDINGS

Lonnie Johnson
- **Lonnie Johnson, Vocals and Instrumentals, 1927–1932 (Origin Jazz Library)**
- **Mr. Johnson's Blues (Mamlish)**
- **The Blues of Lonnie Johnson (Swaggie)**

The Origin has the best and most varied selection of Lonnie Johnson's own music, including both vocals and instrumental showpieces. The Mamlish album reveals Johnson in both starring and supporting roles, backing up such singers as Mooch Richardson, Texas Alexander, and Victoria Spivey on a number of selections. The Swaggie might be most difficult to find but offers perfect clarity of sound on sixteen fine Decca selections, including a remake of the influential "Blue Ghost Blues" and the charming "Got the Blues for the West End" and "Mr. Johnson Swing."

Leroy Carr and Scrapper Blackwell
- **Blues Before Sunrise (Columbia)**
- **Naptown Blues (Yazoo)**
- **Don't Cry When I'm Gone (Flyright)**

The first is undoubtedly the best selection, but it's long out of print. Actually, the Flyright duplicates many of the best Columbia sides (although it is missing "Midnight Hour," "Mean Mistreater Mama," and "Blues Before Sunrise," three of Carr's standards) and adds such indispensable items as "New How Long How Long Blues Part 2" and "Alabama Woman Blues." The Yazoo focuses more on novelty items like "Carried Water for the Elephant," a seemingly autobiographical tale, and "Papa Wants a Cookie," but it, too, provides a good selection of blues. Really, you can't go wrong on any of these records—all are mournful, elegiac, stately, and poignant by turns but never far removed from a good sense of fun.

— 10 —

Chicago
Jump

The logical consequences of a star system in the blues were much the same as they were in the concurrent birth and development of another entertainment industry, the movies: those who controlled the means of production (in this case the record *producers,* the manufacturers) sought more and more to extend that control over exactly what the public was buying. In a very real sense, this foretold exactly what would happen with rock'n'roll, where the success and growth of a lively regional music took the recording industry by surprise, and the recording industry reacted first with shock and dismay, then by turning right around and formularizing the very product for which it had first expressed such loathing.

The result for the blues, and later for rock'n'roll, was twofold. First, with the success of Lonnie Johnson, Leroy Carr, Peetie Wheatstraw, and others, blues became big business. Second, the music itself changed as the record companies, realizing the larger profits to be made, concentrated on those artists most likely to maximize sales and least likely to remain confined to small, difficult-to-approach regional markets. This evolution was complicated by the Depression, which very nearly wrecked the recording industry. (In 1932, overall sales were five percent of what they were in 1927 and, according to blues historian Mike Rowe, total race record sales amounted to no more than 60,000 copies; just five years before, individual releases had been flirting with sales of one million.) The retrenchment that followed came about as a result both of commercial pressures and of what might be termed realistic cost analysis. After the advent of the Depression, no longer did companies go out into the field. A country-blues session like Bukka White's in 1940 was extremely rare, and even Robert Johnson's 1937–1938 sessions for Vocalion were something of a holdover from another era. Talent scouts were no longer combing the countryside for talent, holding auditions in Memphis, Atlanta, Birmingham. At the same time, magnet cities—St. Louis and Chicago, in particular—became thriving recording centers that beckoned to the aspiring bluesman who wanted to consider a serious "career" in the blues.

The Bluebird beat (Bluebird was RCA's race label) was considered predictable, but it reflected the music in clubs and jook joints.
Courtesy of *Living Blues*

Lester Melrose

In Chicago, Lester Melrose, a white music store owner who became a music publisher, virtually controlled the blues industry. Between 1934 and his retirement in 1951, he estimated that he recorded ninety percent of everything that Columbia and RCA put out in their separate, highly successful race series. His close ties with Big Bill Broonzy, Washboard Sam, Jazz Gillum, Tampa Red, Memphis Minnie, Walter Davis, and Sonny Boy Williamson—along with his introduction to more rural bluesmen like Big Joe Williams, Arthur Crudup, and Tommy McClennan through his Chicago contacts—virtually insured that he would control the blues recording industry. For these were the reigning kings (and queen) of the blues in the 1930s. Melrose, in fact, put his stamp on virtually every blues recording coming out of Chicago for more than a decade, whether he recorded it himself or it was recorded by competitors in commercial imitation of his work.

In the 1950s and 1960s the blues that had been recorded in Chicago in the decade just before World War II were dismissed in many quarters as being of little value, assembly-line stuff, impure, a bastardized corruption of the real thing. Records from this era were said, pejoratively, to possess "that Bluebird beat" (Bluebird was the RCA budget label, and the beat was considered to be predictable, metronomic, and contrary to the blues' free spirit), and one title was held to be virtually indistinguishable from another. In some ways this criticism was undoubtedly justified, for there did come to be a certain sameness to Lester Melrose's approach, as an interchangeable group of musicians played on each other's recordings and formed the blues' first loosely structured studio group. At the same time, performers like Big Bill, Sonny Boy Williamson, and Tampa Red achieved a professionalism and a musical sophistication that had eluded all but the most determined country bluesmen (Robert Johnson is one prominent exception), and the use of a band in the studio was in many ways more true to conditions in the Chicago clubs—and even the country jook joints—that had become the primary forum for the blues. There is no doubt that singers like Muddy Waters and Howlin' Wolf injected new life into a formula that had gone stale after World War II, but there is equally little doubt that artists like Sonny Boy Williamson and Tampa Red in particular provided musical and personal role models to the younger men as well as a specific blueprint for the band style that would transform the Chicago blues.

Tampa Red

Tampa Red was the first of the Chicago blues stars, a shy, quiet man, according to his contemporaries, who ran a roominghouse and rehearsal hall all through the 1930s and 1940s and provided support to every up-and-coming bluesman who came to the city. He was born Hudson Whittaker (or Woodbridge) in Georgia around 1900 and grew up in Tampa, eventually joining Ma Rainey's traveling show, where he met his piano-playing partner, Georgia Tom Dorsey (later to become one of the most successful gospel songwriters and publishers in the world). Together they followed the piano-guitar success of "How Long How Long Blues" with their own "It's Tight Like That," a throwaway piece of lightly intended double-entendre material that was recorded three months after the Leroy Carr hit, in September 1928. Like "How Long How Long," "It's Tight Like That" became the rage, sold hundreds of thousands of copies, went through numerous versions, adaptations, and imitations, and established a whole new trend in songs—in this case "hokum," a light-hearted party-time genre that has never completely disappeared. Tampa Red, however, was more than a hokum singer. Billed as "The Guitar Wizard" and sharing billing with his "Golden Guitar," Tampa Red was one of the smoothest and most influential of slide guitarists, providing a direct model for Robert Nighthawk and exerting a good deal of influence even on such country stalwarts as Muddy Waters. He sang in a syrupy, somewhat adenoidal voice that was a little reminiscent of Lonnie Johnson, with whom he also shared an affinity for crooning popular melodies. Like Leroy Carr, he authored a good number of blues standards, like "Sweet Little Angel," "It Hurts Me, Too," "Don't You Lie to Me," "Love Her With a Feeling," and many more, which were eventually recorded by B.B. King, Robert Nighthawk, Chuck Berry, and Elmore James, among others. In addition, Tampa Red extended the concept of the piano-guitar duet into a quasi-band setting, taking up first with Big Maceo and later with Maceo's student (and Otis Spann's contemporary), Johnnie Jones. In fact, it was with Maceo that Tampa Red set the standard for the dynamic relationship between piano and guitar that was at the heart of the great Muddy Waters bands of the 1950s, and with Maceo he made some of the most propulsive jump music prior to the advent of rhythm and blues.

Big Maceo

Apart from Otis Spann, Muddy's long-time accompanist and a stalwart soloist in his own right, Big Maceo was the greatest of the blues piano players. Born Major Merriweather in Texas in 1905, he came to Detroit at the age of thirty, split a session with Tampa Red in June, 1941, and saw his first release, "Worried Life Blues," (a wistful adaptation of Sleepy John Estes's "Someday Baby") become an immediate hit and an all-time blues standard. Although he never repeated the commercial success of that first record, Maceo went on to establish himself as a premier blues and boogie woogie piano man, bringing together in curious combination a husky, wispy, almost forlorn sort of voice and a piano technique that could alternate the most melancholy blues with a hammering, two-fisted stomp without ever missing a beat. It cannot really be said that he exerted an enormous influence, for while blues piano was present from the beginning of recorded blues, there have been very few major blues *singers* who have focused primarily on piano (Sunnyland Slim is perhaps one, Peetie Wheatstraw another, though only Leroy Carr, whose pianistic style was not nearly as distinguished as Maceo's, fully captured the melancholy of the blues). Maceo was, however, the explicit model for both Johnnie Jones and Otis Spann, the two great piano bluesmen in postwar Chicago, both of whom claimed to have played right hand for Maceo on record after he suffered a debilitating stroke in 1946. Maceo continued to record off and on until his death in 1953, but never again was he physically able to attain the heights of the magnificent sides he recorded over a brief five-year period.

Big Bill Broonzy

There were many other prominent piano players in Chicago, for piano was very much a staple of the Chicago blues band, but most were studio musicians and there were no other major front men to speak of. Black Bob, Bob Call, Josh Altheimer, Blind John Davis were the ones who played most frequently on the Lester Melrose sessions, and all played regularly with Big Bill Broonzy, the king of Chicago blues singers in the 1930s. Broonzy, like each of the other Chicago blues stars, was an interesting combination of country and city, outright traditionalism and polished urbanity. Born in 1893 in Mississippi and raised in Arkansas, like many first-generation bluesmen he came out of the country string band tradition and played fiddle and banjo long before he took up guitar. He did not learn to play guitar at all, he states in his autobiography *Big Bill Blues*, until he moved to Chicago in 1920 and learned from Papa Charlie Jackson. He recorded originally in 1926 and 1927 as a hokum and ragtime guitarist very much under the influence of Blind Blake and Tampa Red, but in the 1930s he turned himself around, becoming the very model of the urban bluesman on solo sides, band tracks, and piano-guitar duets that combined the fluency of Scrapper Blackwell's guitar-playing with the mellifluousness of Leroy Carr's vocals. Like Carr—and somewhat unlike Tampa Red or Lonnie Johnson, who could become cloying—Broonzy possessed the gift of taking a folk saying, polishing and refining it, setting it to a recognizable melody, singing in an easy, high-pitched voice that never strained or reached for emotional effects, and coming up with a blues that was seldom stilted or cliched. Broonzy was the center of a whole circle of singers that included his "half-brother" Washboard Sam (Robert Brown), a

*Big Bill Broonzy came out
of the country string band
tradition to become king
of the Chicago blues stars
in the 1930's.*
Courtesy of *Sing Out*

prolific composer and policeman on the side, and Jazz Gillum, a harmonica player of limited technical accomplishments but also a cred-
itable writer and, with Broonzy, often credited as the author of "Key to
the Highway," one of the blues' best-known standards. By all accounts Big Bill Broonzy, along with Sonny Boy Williamson and
Tampa Red, offered a helping hand to any number of up-and-
coming young blues singers, including Muddy Waters, and dominated the Chicago scene for nearly two decades both in the clubs
and in the studio. He continued to record extensively after World War
II and even enjoyed a brief period of revival as a folk singer in the
1950s, traveling to Europe many times, singing in a studied, slow-
paced, arrhythmic manner, almost like a conscious re-creation of
the field hollers of his youth, and reminiscing to his young audience
about a lifetime spent sharecropping. He died of cancer in 1959 but
had earlier written in his autobiography:

"When you write about me, please don't say that I'm a jazz musician. Don't say I'm a musician or a guitar player—just write Big Bill
was a well-known blues singer and player and has recorded 260
blues songs from 1925 up till 1952; he was a happy man when he
was drunk and playing with women; he was liked by all the blues
singers, some would get a little jealous sometimes but Bill would buy
a bottle of whiskey and they all would start laughing and playing
again, Big Bill would get drunk and slip off from the party and go
home to sleep. . . ."

John Lee "Sonny Boy" Williamson

As influential as anyone on the development of the contemporary
Chicago blue style was John Lee Williamson, the *first* Sonny Boy Williamson (an older, Mississippi-born singer named Rice Miller took
Williamson's name and during his lifetime, and after his death the
second Sonny Boy became a major contributor to the postwar Memphis and Chicago sound), who was described by Big Bill, one of his
few competitors for popularity, as "a good-hearted boy, and free-

handed as he could be." What gave Sonny Boy Williamson I his particular significance was that he was the blues' first harmonica star. Though there had been other highly influential accompanists, and soloists like DeFord Bailey and Jaybird Coleman had made records in the early days of field recording, Sonny Boy was the first to become anything like a star in his own right. Born in Jackson, Tennessee, in 1914, and thus part of the generation that spawned Muddy Waters, Robert Johnson, Johnny Shines, and Howlin' Wolf, he came up under the influence of the blues of his fellow Tennesseean Sleepy John Estes and, in fact, when he first recorded, at age twenty-three, it was very much in that rough country vein behind the twin guitars of Big Joe Williams and Robert Nighthawk. He quickly adapted to the emerging Chicago band style, however, and with his astringent harmonica—which was soon to become an indispensable part of the postwar blues band—took the ensemble sound even further than his peers. His singing style has often been described as "tongue-tied" because of a stutter in his speaking voice, and his consequent manner of spitting out the words with a hesitant, almost strangled sort of delivery gave his records a greater intensity, and perhaps a more pronounced idiosyncrasy, than those of Big Bill Broonzy and Tampa Red. Like Big Bill and Tampa, he contributed a disproportionate number of standards to the blues repertoire, among them "Good Morning Little School Girl," "Bluebird Blues," and "Check Up On My Baby," and his murder, at the age of thirty-four, had a chilling effect on the blues community.

When Muddy Waters first came to Chicago, he saw it as something of a closed shop, and it probably was closed, for the most part, to new sounds and old country ways. By 1943 Muddy, just up from Mississippi, was itching to get a start, and he remembers with, perhaps as much feeling as accuracy, "Blues was dying out. There was nothing happening. Well, a few things. Big Maceo and Tampa Red, Sonny Boy Williams, but not too many help you. It was pretty ruggish, man." Within a few years it would all have changed. Sonny Boy would be dead, the band style that had been struggling to emerge would be firmly entrenched, and the rest of the Chicago stars would all be forced to retire or change, as the new, postwar wave of sound rolled in, with new recording companies and new markets to reach.

SELECTED RECORDINGS

— ANTHOLOGIES —

- Blues Roots/Chicago—The 1930s (RBF)
- Windy City Blues: The Transition, 1935–1953 (Nighthawk)
- Lake Michigan Blues, 1934–1941 (Nighthawk)

The RBF Roots album is *the* mainstream album to have. In addition to Big Bill and Memphis Minnie standards, it features Jazz Gillum doing his "Key to the Highway," St. Louis Jimmy with his original "Going Down Slow," Johnnie Temple performing the highly influential "Louise," and nice cuts from Washboard Sam and Big Maceo. Good music, well-programmed, but the sound, as usual with RBF issues, is dull and the selection might be somewhat more adventurous. Which it is on the two Nighthawk albums, classics of the blues anthology genre, which mix not overly familiar titles by John Lee "Sonny Boy" Williamson and Robert Nighthawk with unfamiliar artists like Tampa Kid and Elijah Jones to create an overall pastiche of brilliant, varied, and surprising music. **Lake Michigan Blues** is dominated by the sound of Robert Nighthawk and Sonny Boy Williamson in particular, with six sides from the extraordinary 1937 session that they shared with Big Joe Williams (this was the record debut for both Nighthawk and Sonny Boy). In addition there are a couple of exemplary sides by Tampa Red and his imitator, Tampa Kid, and Robert Jr. Lockwood's "Little Boy Blue," one of the most eloquent transliterations of the Robert Johnson style on record. **Windy City Blues** carries on with two additional titles from Lockwood's first session, a couple more Tennessee-flavored numbers by Sonny Boy Williamson, and an entire side of postwar cuts by bluesmen like Lockwood, Tampa Red, and Johnny Shines, adapting a traditional music to the new amplified sound.

—— INDIVIDUAL ARTISTS ——

Tampa Red
- **Tampa Red: The Guitar Wizard (RCA: two-record set)**
- **Tampa Red: The Guitar Wizard (Blues Classics)**

Two exemplary albums with the same title and separate liner notes by Jim O'Neal that should serve as a model of clarity, feeling, and information. The RCA issue, now out of print, spans the length of Tampa Red's career and the breadth of his repertoire, from his deepest blues like "Crying Won't Help You" and "It Hurts Me Too," two staples of the latter-day downhome Mississippi style, to pop take-offs like "Give It Up Buddy and Get Goin'," "When You Were a Girl of Seven," and "When I Take My Vacation in Harlem." Just as varied, just as marvelous, and just as instructive about the evolution of the Chicago blues band style is the Blues Classics album, which also covers the period from the mid-1930s to 1953, and features hard blues, novelty material, wonderful instrumentation, and such titles as "Let Me Play With Your Poodle," "Sweet Little Angel," and "She Wants to Sell My Monkey." Good times and good music.

Big Maceo
- **Chicago Breakdown (RCA: two-record set)**

A nonpareil offering. Nothing can compare with this double-record set, comprising much of Maceo's piano-blues output for Bluebird. There are slow, deeply felt blues, there are the "Texas Stomp," "Detroit Jump," and "Chicago Breakdown"—all storming instrumentals, there is subtle, sensitive accompaniment, mostly from Tampa Red. Most of all, there is that ineffable sense of sweetness that is at the heart of Big Maceo's recordings, the soft, almost feathery voice set against that rumbling left hand, and the overall effect of sad, lost, and lonely poignancy.

Big Bill Broonzy
- **Big Bill Broonzy: 1932–1942 (Biograph)**
- **Big Bill's Blues (Epic)**
- **Big Bill and Sonny Boy (English RCA)**

The best of the Big Bill selections. My favorite is **Big Bill's Blues**, but Broonzy is so smooth and consistent a performer that you can't go wrong with any of these. All three albums feature varied and interesting accompaniment (including trumpet and sax). **Big Bill's Blues** contains some of his best and most familiar compositions, and the English issue includes an exemplary side by Big Bill and an equally exemplary one by Sonny Boy. For early Big Bill Broonzy, Yazoo has primarily ragtime albums of somewhat limited interest. For Big Bill as folksinger (mid-to-late 1950s) Folkways has the best selection, including some nice interview material with Studs Terkel.

Sonny Boy Williamson
■ **Sonny Boy Williamson Vols. 1–3 (Blues Classics)**

In addition to the half album by English RCA listed above, these offer the best selection. Like Big Bill Broonzy, Sonny Boy was an amazingly prolific artist and a remarkably consistent one as well. Of these three albums, my favorite is the second, but I'm not sure quite what distinguishes it from the other two, other than the original versions of such familiar songs as "Hoodoo Man," "Stop Breaking Down" (a variant on Robert Johnson's composition), and "Shake the Boogie," and a pure country, Brownsville-laced "Skinny Woman," which comes from his very first session. My least favorite of the three is the third album, but again I have no solid reasons except that it seems more transitional and middle-of-the-road to me, without the forcefulness of some of the later sides or the innocence of the earlier ones. Any of these records gives a good representation of Sonny Boy, though, and personal taste will find a favorite.

The War Is Over: Around the World and Home Again

What happened to blues recording after World War II was an explosion roughly parallel to the social explosion taking place in the postwar world. Many plausible explanations have been advanced to account for this recrudescence—the rough, jagged music mirrored the dislocations of postwar society, migrants to the city were homesick for the South—but perhaps the best has to do with business. Very simply, the blues recording industry virtually shut down in 1942, under the combined influences of the Petrillo recording ban (James Petrillo, head of the musicians' union, issued the ban ostensibly to counter the threat of the jukebox to the musician's livelihood) and wartime rationing of shellac. While records did continue to be issued, they were far fewer in number and for the most part were decidedly not blues. With the reemergence of recording, the major companies (RCA, Columbia) were slow to pick up their blues and hillbilly lines. Swing, pop, jump music were all popular on a mass scale, but even distribution methods had changed, and it may have been too much trouble to set up the mom-and-pop outlets, the traditional blues distribution network, all over again. Or perhaps it was simply that tastes had changed, and recording technology was more widely available. In any case, in the five or ten years after the war there emerged an astonishing number and variety of independent labels—from Duke, Aladdin, Specialty, King to Chess, Sun, Modern, and Vee Jay. It was these companies, and smaller, less well-known ones, that led the way in blues and rhythm and blues recording and produced the last great wave of downhome recording before television made regionalism a dead word.

Blues Radio

One other factor should be mentioned with regard to the dissemination of blues, and that is radio. All through the 1920s and 1930s, blues remained virtually unexposed on the radio. While hillbilly music had its Grand Ole Opry and even before that, Chicago's WLS Jamboree, and while a whole recording industry was able to spring up

Sonny Boy Williamson II (Rice Miller) got national exposure on the King Biscuit show, which was the first to offer blues performers a regular radio outlet.
Courtesy of *Living Blues*

around the faithful Saturday-night listening habits of a national audience, blues was far more localized in its distribution and effect. Robert Johnson, it's true, was able to do a few broadcasts on the Elder Moten Hour in Detroit around 1937, and Lonnie Johnson had his own radio show in New York in 1929, but it was not until the advent of the King Biscuit Show in Helena, Arkansas (a real hotbed of the downhome blues) in 1941 that blues singers had access to the airwaves on a regular basis. This was the show that made Rice Miller, the second Sonny Boy Williamson, something more than a shadowy local legend, gave Robert Jr. Lockwood his start, and served as the model for the innumerable farm and feed broadcasts that sprang up both before and after World War II and featured such local stars as B.B. King, Howlin' Wolf, Elmore James, and even Muddy Waters. Eventually, in 1948, Memphis's WDIA became the first all-black station, the self-styled Mother Station of the Negro, and provided an outlet of incalculable importance for blues stars and blues recordings. The point is, radio was able to elevate local tradition into something that could reach more than just a few listeners at a time, even without the aid of records (the second Sonny Boy Williamson did not record for more than a decade after his first broadcasts, even though he was a familiar figure all through the South as a result of them). Radio also confounded local tradition at the same time, making it possible for a young bluesman like B.B. King, who got his start as salesman, DJ, and live entertainer on WDIA, to absorb the influence not just of his uncle Bukka White but of Django Reinhardt, Charlie Christian, and blues shouters like Roy Brown and Wynonie Harris as well.

Rhythm and blues

The result of both the recording boom—which for the first time reinstituted the process of field recording as well as encouraging a vigorous search for talent—and the fresh exposure to music far beyond any local tradition was the growth of a number of different blues traditions. Probably the most popular was the rhythm and blues, which would evolve most directly into rock and roll and which sprang out of the jump bands of trained musicians like Lucky Millinder and Buddy Johnson. For the purposes of this book, it's possible only to gloss over this rich hybrid, which, while clearly derived from the blues' classic traditions, established new traditions of its own and has dated somewhat in the manner of women's blues of the 1920s, with elegant, sophisticated, and "modern" arrangements coming across pretty much like the bygone finery of any era.

Basically, though, rhythm and blues represented a two-pronged tradition. On the rhythm side, many of the great shouters emerged or came into their own just around the time of World War II. Big Joe Turner came out of Kansas City in the 1930s and ended up as one of the great rock'n'rollers, with a big-voiced shouting style that was equally well-adapted to blues or rock. Of the younger stand-up singers, by far the most popular were Wynonie "Mr. Blues" Harris, who started out as a vocalist in the jump band of Lucky Millinder; Roy Brown, who wrote the rhythm and blues and rock'n'roll cornerstone "Good Rockin' Tonight" and introduced the "crying" style that became so popular in the 1950s; and, of course, Louis Jordan, leader of the Tympany Five (often Seven), who combined jazz, comedy, and blues to carry on the minstrel tradition and provide a perfect model for rock'n'roll's first stars, Bill Haley and his Comets.

On the ballad side, rhythm and blues took its cue from the more mannered "cocktail blues" of Nat King Cole, whose great trio recordings provided both a model and an inspiration for a whole school of "soft" blues that included pianists Charles Brown, Amos Milburn, and—almost slavishly at the beginning of his career—Ray Charles. This was considered a much classier brand of blues than the downhome variety, and it was the kind of blues that Muddy Waters, for example, was expected to be able to play when he first arrived in Chicago in 1943. Sales were always much higher for this uptown brand of blues—jump and ballad variety—and yet on the downhome side blues entered a state of ferment just as great as soon as its commercial potential became apparent.

For while downhome blues was never as popular as the uptown sound, it was definitely cheaper to record, and so many of the new record companies, which were at best shoestring operations, began to specialize in a sound that their owners had probably never even imagined. In many cases the talent came to them; in some, it showed up on their sales swings through the Deep South, as they peddled records from the back of a car and cemented personal contacts that would set the course of postwar blues and rhythm and blues recording. It was a wild and woolly time for daring entrepreneurs, almost all of them first or second generation Jewish immigrants, each competing to beat the other to a music that must have seemed no less foreign, and no less intriguing, than the whole American experience. It was the age of the independent operator in every respect.

Meanwhile, the two great waves of downhome blues were migrating in altogether opposite directions. To put it in crudely oversimplified terms: Mississippi blues was heading north, to Memphis and then on to Detroit and Chicago. Texas blues, on the other hand, which had gone largely unrecorded from the Depression on (blues historian Paul Oliver suggests that one of the reasons was, quite simply, that Dallas was twice as far from recording centers like Chicago and New York as Memphis, say), suddenly exploded on the recording scene with the massive migration of blacks from the Texas-Louisiana area to the West Coast. In 1930, there were 80,000 blacks in California; by 1950, after the spectacular growth of wartime defense industries, there were 460,000, most from Texas, Louisiana, and Oklahoma. With the rise of the West Coast independent record labels, it was only natural that Texas blues should emerge as a dominant force. And with the rise of Texas blues, Sam "Lightnin' " Hopkins emerged as one of the leading exponents of the downhome blues.

Lightnin' Hopkins

Lightnin' Hopkins we met already as an eight-year-old knocked out by the music of Blind Lemon Jefferson at a picnic in Buffalo, Texas, in 1920. He was a cousin of Texas Alexander and accompanied the older man frequently all through the 1930s and 1940s. By the time he finally got to record for Aladdin in 1946, he was a familiar figure around Houston and was teamed with piano player Wilson "Thunder" Smith for his West Coast session. That was how he came to be called Lightnin', that was where he came to sing the first of his songs about each of his various wives ("Katie Mae" and "Ida Mae" and "Miss Loretta" and "Glory Bee"), and that was how he came to have his first hit. He went on to record scores of songs, first for Aladdin, then for Bill Quinn's Gold Star label in Houston, then for literally dozens of other companies between 1946 and 1954. He was never a big star in a national sense, and he never really had a Top Ten hit, but around Houston he was a celebrity of the first order, and he recorded every kind of Texas blues there was, documenting the various traditions that Blind Lemon Jefferson had first indicated and establishing a personal, and often autobiographical, genre of his own. His guitar was an extension of his voice, much in the manner of earlier Texas singers, with the repetitive pattern of a thumb plucking at the bass strings often the only accompaniment to the vocal portions of his songs. The instrumental passages highlighted powerful sweeping chords and highly ornamental single-string runs, and, in Muddy Waters's assessment, his voice exemplified the deep blues that Muddy himself most values. There is a cracked, leathery, almost sardonic quality to it, the side-of-the mouth manner of the street hustler combined with the open emotional expression of the most deeply personal blues (Lightnin' often alternates a recitative patter with a sung chorus that gets at the emotional meat of the song). Lightnin' is a

Lightnin' Hopkins, who spearheaded the downhome blues revival, extended the Texas traditions that Blind Lemon Jefferson had exemplified.
Courtesy of Chris Strachwitz/
Arhoolie Records

gambler, an egocentric, a man fearful of responsibility, and a poet, and it all comes through in his songs, which are products of the moment more often than not, sudden bursts of inspiration, whimsy of the highest order.

The popularity of Lightnin' Hopkins, and the availability of so many of his records, in many ways provided the spearhead for the revival of interest in the downhome sound in general. Muddy Waters would not begin recording for Chess for another year, or have his first hit until nearly two years after Lightnin' Hopkins's first session. John Lee Hooker's "Boogie Chillen" did not come out until November of 1948. The records that Lightnin' made, and the sales that they chalked up, were just two of the factors that proved that a market definitely did exist.

That market soon accommodated a number of remarkable Texas bluesmen, among them Smokey Hogg, Lil Son Jackson, Frankie Lee Sims, and an adoptive Texan, Lowell Fulson. Of these, Hogg was the only one to have recorded before World War II (he cut two sides in 1937) and was probably the most mainstream stylist as well, singing for the most part in lazy Peetie Wheatstraw-influenced fashion, with a smooth drawling delivery, falsetto interpolations, pronounced rhythmic eccentricity (there is never any beat as such to Smokey Hogg's music, though a pulse can sometimes be detected), and an occasional reminder of Texas Alexander's penitentiary moans. Lil Son Jackson, on the other hand, clung more closely to the nervous rhythms of prewar Texas blues, while Frankie Lee Sims crashed headlong into the churning waters of rock'n'roll (actually Jackson may have *named* rock'n'roll with his one big hit, a 1951 adaptation of "Rock Me, Mama" called "Rockin' and Rollin' "). All three of these singers add something to the heritage of Texas blues, but more significant as an artist in his own right is Oklahoman Lowell Fulson.

Lowell Fulson

Fulson, born in Tulsa in 1921 of mixed black and Indian parentage, comes from the most varied and heterogenous musical background. He started out as a teenager playing country music with a white string band, hooked up with Texas Alexander in the late 1930s, and ended up in California when he mustered out of the Navy in 1945. There he began recording in the sophisticated trio style popularized by fellow Texans Charles Brown and Amos Milburn, with strong single-string lead work modeled on the dominant mode of T-Bone Walker. At the same time he recorded a series of numbers with only his brother Martin seconding him on guitar, which represent some of the most memorable postwar country-blues performances. These include not only traditional songs like "River Blues" (an offshoot of various "Penitentiary Blues" recorded by Lightnin' Hopkins, Smokey Hogg, and Texas Alexander) but also plangent contemporary numbers like "Three O'Clock Blues," which later became a standard for B.B. King, as did King's adaptation of Fulson's "Every Day I Have the Blues." Fulson went on to form various orchestras that included Earl Brown on alto, Stanley Turrentine and Fathead Newman on tenor, and Ray Charles on piano, and proved remarkably adaptable to the various rhythm and blues trends that came along, producing hits for a period of over twenty years and enjoying Top Ten success as late as 1966 with his version of Jimmy McCracklin's "Tramp." His voice never lost its thin, tensile strength nor his guitar its distinctive Texas flavor. Whatever the genre, you could always recognize Lowell Fulson wrapping his voice around the lyrics, coaxing a *sound* out of the words, summoning up something of the spare, elegant style that has characterized the Texas blues in its own sinuous fashion over the last sixty or seventy-five years.

John Lee Hooker

The Mississippi blues, on the other hand, continued to pursue a more straightforward and more easily delineated line. Although it is possible to find examples of Mississippi blues on the West Coast, for the most part the migration—both of people and of style—followed a more direct route, first to Memphis and then on to Chicago. John Lee Hooker was one of the few well-known bluesmen who did not either stop in Memphis or make the second half of the journey. Hooker came to Memphis from Clarksdale, Mississippi, where he grew up with Muddy Waters, who was two years his senior. After spending a year or two working as a janitor at the W.C. Handy Theater on Beale Street in Memphis, he went on to Cincinnati, then Detroit, and never got to Chicago at all. Actually, this was not so uncommon a route, but because there never was a Detroit recording industry to rival that of Chicago or a single label to rival Chess, Vee Jay, or even the lesser Chicago companies, John Lee Hooker was the only certifiable star to emerge out of Detroit, and even then primarily on West Coast (Modern) and Chicago (Chess and Vee Jay) labels for his big hits.

If Lightnin' Hopkins was something of a throwback, John Lee Hooker was a complete anachronism. Except for his amplified guitar, Hooker might very well have been recorded fifty years earlier. His blues were the undiluted blues of Mississippi, solo sides for the most part at the beginning, modal chants more than melodic "songs," characterized by unrhymed, seemingly unpolished lyrics, a dark coloration to the voice, a fierce attack (but rarely a changed chord) on the guitar, and a relentlessly pounding foot to provide the beat. None of these elements even remotely resembled a modern approach to the blues. And yet with his first release, "Boogie Chillen," John Lee Hooker achieved one of the biggest hits of the postwar era and one of its most enduring and most imitated standards as well. As a solo act, Hooker recorded for an astonishing number of labels under a wide variety of pseudonyms. Eventually, in the 1950s, he started recording with a band, though never with one that found a style to fit the unchanging, unvarying drama of his modal chants, the unpredictable bursts of his guitar, and his idiosyncratic approach to meter. Nonetheless, he continued to have hits, recording in fully as many modes for fully as many labels as Lightnin' Hopkins. At the Newport Folk Festival he was a folk singer, playing an acoustic guitar with stand-up bass for accompaniment; on the rhythm and blues front, he had a Top Twenty hit with "Boom Boom" in 1962; rock'n'roll groups like the Animals and the Rolling Stones adapted some of his most familiar songs and transformed them into rock'n'roll classics with little apparent effort. In recent years, when boogie has really come into style, John Lee Hooker has become something of a legend, and some of his earlier, more introspective work has been lost sight of, but always he has retained the essential core of himself—the Boogie Man appellation cuts both ways, and the music lies somewhere between a dream and a nightmare.

Sam Phillips and the Memphis Sound

Memphis is probably the place where the boogie first came from. Though Hooker recorded before the Memphis boogie was ever put down on record, it seems likely that he picked up his characteristic sound—or at least the overlay of his sound—from his stay in Memphis. For this is very much what we hear, on record after record, coming out of Memphis in the early 1950s: brash, danceable rhythms, guitar overamplified to the point of distortion, classic boogie lyrics brighter and more outgoing perhaps than Hooker's, with less of a primitive undertow, but clearly mining the same territory. The man responsible for recording this music for the first time after World War II—and the man responsible for the birth of rock'n'roll, another Memphis invention—was Sam Phillips. Phillips, a radio engineer from Florence, Alabama, was working at station WREC when he built his own little studio in a converted radiator shop on Union Avenue. His aim, he told a trade reporter from *Billboard* at the time, was to provide a place to record "the great Negro artists . . . when Negro artists in the South who wanted to make a record just had no place to go." This is what he did. Some of the first Negro artists that he recorded, not for his own label but for leasing to the Modern label on the West Coast and the Chess label in Chicago, were B.B. King, Howlin' Wolf, Bobby Bland, and Junior Parker. Ike Turner, a teenaged follower of the jump bands from Clarksdale, Mississippi and a capable piano and guitar player as well, served as his talent scout, and the world rapidly became his audience.

When Howlin' Wolf moved to West Memphis in 1948, he had no intention of making records. He was thirty-eight years old, had lived on a farm all his life, and it was just the prospect of better pay and shorter hours that lured him to the city. "Back in the country you'd

John Lee Hooker played the undiluted (if electrified) blues of Mississippi, and yet had an impressive list of hits.
Courtesy of *Living Blues*

work all night for a fish sandwich, glad to get it, too. In Memphis I started to really get somewhere." Within a year he had not only formed his own band but, like B.B. King, Rufus Thomas, Sonny Boy Williamson (Rice Miller), and Joe Hill Louis the Be-Bop Boy and His One Man Band, he had his own radio show. It was a fifteen-minute spot sponsored by a local grain company and broadcast over station KWEM in West Memphis. It was undoubtedly because of the exposure he got on the radio that he, like each of the others, first got to record.

He was recorded around 1950 by Sam Phillips for RPM, a subsidiary of Joe and Jules Bihari's Los Angeles-based Modern label. The Biharis, like the Chess brothers in Chicago, first got into the record business through the jukeboxes. Their label grew directly out of a jukebox-supply operation and, like Chess, was originally oriented toward be-bop and big-band sound. Like Chess, too, they sensed a need that wasn't being filled by the major companies, and when they leased and put out "Boogie Chillen," which had been recorded by Bernie Besman, another small-time entrepreneur from Detroit, they were committed irrevocably to the blues.

Sam Phillips recorded the very best in Memphis blues for both Chess and RPM, often leasing different takes of the same tune to the two companies. He recorded classic harmonica sides by Walter Horton, frenzied boogies by Joe Hill Louis and Willie Nix, and *sui generis* music by the Howlin' Wolf, one of the giants of the postwar blues world. He recorded raw jump blues by Rosco Gordon and His Orchestra and various manifestations of Ike Turner's Kings of Rhythm (including Jackie Brenston, Turner's baritone saxophonist, doing "Rocket 88," a huge seller for Chess and often called the first true rock'n'roll hit because of its preoccupation with fast cars, fast women, and a solid beat). At the radio station where he worked, Sam

Phillips was frequently met by fellow workers with greetings like: "Well, you smell okay, I guess you haven't been hanging around those niggers today." But he kept on recording sides for both Chess and RPM, pretty much according to his own lights, until the two companies got into a fight over Howlin' Wolf's contract. "I was just a country boy," said Wolf, "glad to get some sounds on wax. I didn't know what was happening, but Chess sent a man down to straighten me out. He signed me to a contract, took me up north, put me in the union, and next time I got back to West Memphis I was working a job there." "When Leonard Chess came down here and promised him the moon," remarked Phillips, "it broke my heart. This was one of the things that made me want to start my own label."

Not long afterwards, towards the end of 1951, Sam Phillips did start his own label, Sun Records, which for its first two years concentrated almost exclusively on the black artists Phillips had been recording for others up until then. The sound was the one that Phillips had pioneered, a rocking beat, buzzing guitar sound (legend has it that Phillips broke more than one amplifier just to get the feel he wanted), and much the same echo effect—known as "slap-back" in Phillips's application—that Leonard Chess was striving for in Chicago. There was no question that Sam Phillips was recording the downhome blues sound, but the result was altogether different from the crude homemade recordings cut by John Lee Hooker in Detroit or the offerings of many of the little West Coast labels, where the artist was forced to triumph over audio shortcomings and glaring technical inadequacies. Phillips's recordings were crisp and clear; he never forgot his training as a radio engineer, and he never lost his feeling for musical or individual uniqueness. Whether it was the one-man band of Doctor Ross singing about the boogie disease ("I'm gonna boogie for the doctor, boogie for the nurse/Gonna keep on boogieing/Till they put me in the hearse") or the more sophisticated stylings of the Beale Streeters, a loose aggregation that, at one time or another, included Johnny Ale, Rosco Gordon, Bobby Bland, and B.B. King, Phillips stuck to his fundamental belief. "My mission was to bring out of a person what was in him, to recognize that individual's unique quality and then to find the key to unlock it. . . . My greatest contribution, I think, was to open up an area of freedom within the artist himself, to help him to express what he believed his message to be."

Memphis in the 1950s was an incredible cauldron of musical activity, rivaled only by New Orleans for its variety of music and by Chicago for the intensity of its blues feeling. Probably never before had there been the creative interaction of so many different black styles, and that interaction—and its concomitant commercial success— might very well still be going on today if Elvis Presley had not walked into the Sun studio after graduating from high school in 1953, to make a birthday recording for his mother. When Sam Phillips eventually recorded him for the Sun label, in June of 1954, the resulting explosion virtually obliterated the race market and brought to a halt the recording of blues in Memphis. As Rufus Thomas said of Phillips, "When Elvis come along, just like he catered to black, he cut it off and went to white. No more blacks did he pick up at all." Despite his high regard for Elvis Presley, Jerry Lee Lewis, Johnny Cash, Carl

Perkins and the rest of his stable of first generation rock'n'rollers (all in one way or another realizations of his vision of "a white man who had the Negro sound and the Negro feel"), Phillips continues to this day to express mixed feelings about swerving from his original path. "This is a regrettable thing on my part, but I saw what I was doing as not deserting the black man—God knows, there was no way I could do that—[but] I saw what I was trying to do with white men was to broaden the base. . . ." Indeed, Elvis Presley went on to record Little Junior Parker's "Mystery Train" as well as Roy Brown's "Good Rocking Tonight" and, some years later, Rufus Thomas's "Tiger Man (King of the Jungle)," all in authentic, authentically felt blues versions. As for Chester Burnett, the Howlin' Wolf, Phillips has said, "I just thought he was the most different singer in the world. His voice was so 'extremely bad' that it fascinated me. Had I not been beaten out of him, there's no telling how many hit records I would have cut with this man. He should have been a pop smash." He would have been bigger than Little Richard or Chuck Berry, according to Sam Phillips, but instead he went to Chicago, where Muddy Waters, an arch-rival even then ("Muddy never did play in West Memphis much, because I was living there . . . but I never did quit trying to be friends," said Wolf disingenuously), secured him his first job. Because by then, Muddy Waters was undisputed king of the Chicago blues, occupying much the same position that Big Bill Broonzy had held when Muddy himself first came to Chicago in 1943.

SELECTED RECORDINGS

— JUMP BLUES —

Big Joe Turner
■ **Early Big Joe (MCA)**
■ **Joe Turner: His Greatest Recordings (Atlantic)**
    There are countless Big Joe Turner recordings, and countless good ones. These are some of the earliest (the MCA volume) and some of the best. **Early Big Joe** features piano accompaniment from such stalwarts as Art Tatum, Willie "The Lion" Smith, and Turner's long-time partner Pete Johnson on many of Big Joe's classic tunes. Sound is not particularly good, but the selection is fine. What I like best about the Atlantic album is that it forces a variety on Big Joe, who is the kind of vocalist who could go all night with a single tune, pouring on the rhythm, turning up verse after indiscriminate verse, but rarely changing the mood. On these seminal rock'n'roll sides ("Shake, Rattle & Roll," "Corrine Corrina," "Honey Hush,") the accompaniment and the mood are meticulously chosen, and Big Joe rides as he never has before or since.

Wynonie Harris
■ **Mr. Blues Is Coming to Town (Route 66)**
■ **Good Rockin' Blues (Gusto/King: two-record set)**
    More of an acquired taste than Turner, though Harris was at least equally influential. Where Turner proved his adeptness at ballads as well as jump tunes, Wynonie Harris was pretty much of a shouter all the way. He was described as possessing "vocal chords seemingly made of steel," and that's the way he comes across. **Mr. Blues Is Coming to Town**, like all Route 66 productions, is beautifully pack-

aged, programmed, selected, and presented and is certainly the album to get, except for the fact that the shoddily put together Gusto/King double set has the hits. Unless you're interested in pure history, stick to the Route 66 for an introduction; it's more listenable and informative in every way. Then, if you're drawn to **Mr. Blues**, go to the King, which has a plethora of novelty material, including a couple of country-and-western tunes, as well as the certifiable hits.

Roy Brown
- **Laughing but Crying (Route 66)**
- **Good Rocking Tonight (Route 66)**
- **Hard Luck Blues (Gusto/King: two-record set)**

The same comments apply here as above, except that the Gusto/King double album is a much more palatable musical package than the Wynonie Harris set. Roy Brown sang in a unique crying style that was almost revolutionary when first introduced and then set the model for B.B. King, Little Richard, James Brown, Bobby Bland, and countless others. His plummy tone and hyperdramatic style are not everyone's meat, but the Route 66 label has set about almost religiously to document this goodtime style, and their Roy Brown albums should be models for how to present a music you love—with good sound, rare illustrations, and good selection of hard blues, rocking blues, and party blues (novelty songs). **Hard Luck Blues** is not far removed in musical quality—it is not removed at all, actually—and that is real tribute to Brown's consistency as a performer.

Louis Jordan
- **The Best of Louis Jordan (MCA)**
- **Greatest Hits Vol.2 1941–1947 (French MCA)**

The clown prince of the blues—good musicianship, good-humored delivery, good jokes, good titles ("Ain't Nobody Here But Us Chickens," "Saturday Night Fish Fry," "Is You Is, Or Is You Ain't My Baby"). Much more easygoing than any of the shouters discussed above, Jordan was not strictly a shouter but an entertainer from the vaudeville tradition with strong roots in blues and jazz. These two albums give the full range of his music—with blues, novelty songs, and his own alto playing getting equal billing—and clearly delineate, in the stylized vocal delivery, why B.B. King, Ray Charles, and Chuck Berry cite him as one of their prime influences and why elements of his repertoire keep turning up not only in their recordings ("Caledonia," "Early in the Mornin' ") but in the standard recordings of countless other contemporary bluesmen as well.

POSTWAR TEXAS
ANTHOLOGIES
- **Texas Blues Vols. 1 and 2 (Arhoolie)**
- **Texas Blues: The Early '50s (Blues Classics)**

A far cry from any of the albums discussed thus far, though it was all going on at the same time. These three albums represent the best of the Texas country blues and are dominated by one man in particular—either his songs or his influence—Lightnin' Hopkins. Vol. 1 and the Blues Classics album (actually the third in the series) are probably the two to get, with classic early sides by Lightnin', Lil

Son Jackson, Lightnin's partner Thunder Smith, and his virtual disciple L.C. Williams on the first, and more of the same plus a good cross-section of a number of other Texas styles (Smokey Hogg, Mercy Dee, Frankie Lee Sims) on the other. Vol. 2 is not far removed in displaying a variety of Texas styles, but its 1960s recordings are not all up to the standard of the original versions, and it has nothing as revelatory as Mance Lipscomb's bitter "Tom Moore's Farm" or Smokey Hogg's "Penitentiary Blues."

- **Texas Blues (United)**
- **Down Behind the Rise (Nighthawk)**

Two exemplary collections in two quite different ways. Both feature the eccentric work of Jesse "Babyface" Thomas (Ramblin' Thomas's brother), who first recorded in 1929 but put together his own quirky, jazz-inflected but solidly Texas-based style after World War II. The Nighthawk album is dominated by Thomas and amounts to a major retrospective of a very underappreciated artist. There are six titles here, ranging in style from the sophisticated pop swing and playful lyrics of "Double D Due Love You" to the lowdown blues. Lightnin' Hopkins, Frankie Lee Sims accompanied by steel guitar, and Wright Holmes, about as fierce and individual a stylist as there is among the Texas singers, are also featured in this thoroughly surprising, thoroughly engrossing collection. **Texas Blues** offers three more titles by Jesse Thomas but is generally more mainstream, with fine selections by Lil Son Jackson, Smokey Hogg, Whistling Alex Moore, and Lowell Fulson. A little more random than the Arhoolie and Blues Classics albums, and definitely less striking than the Nighthawk album, **Texas Blues** nonetheless presents a good cross-section of excellent performances.

INDIVIDUAL PERFORMERS

Lightnin' Hopkins
- **Early Recordings, Vols. 1 and 2 (Arhoolie)**
- **The Blues (Mainstream)**
- **The Roots of Lightnin' Hopkins (Folkways)**
- **How Many More Years I Got? (Fantasy)**

It's hard to know where to begin with Lightnin' Hopkins. Lightnin' can be inspired, and Lightnin' can be workmanlike to the point of dullness. On each of these albums, I think he is inspired, and they provide a good overview of his career, from his earliest recordings to some of his best later ones. I'm sure there are others that could be put forward just as well, but these are my favorites.

The two Arhoolie albums represent not only the best of his early work at Bill Quinn's Gold Star Studio, they are also among the most accessible of these albums. Vol. 2 in particular offers alternate takes, previously unissued recordings, and some of his very best individual titles, but the two records make a set that can stand with the testament of any individual bluesman. **The Blues** represents Lightnin' in mid-career and is also commonly available. Once titled "Last of the Great Blues Singers," it was recorded in the early 1950s for the West Coast label SIW, and included some of his best, most affecting, and seemingly most freely improvised commercial sides. **The Roots of Lightnin' Hopkins** was Lightnin's 1959 "rediscovery" album and perhaps for that reason has always occupied a fond spot in my heart. It includes a spoken reminiscence of Blind Lemon, the traditional "Penitentiary Blues" and Lemon's "See That My Grave Is Kept Clean," with additional improvised blues and boogies, all sung to the accompaniment of an acoustic guitar. It's as exciting to me now as it was when I heard it on first release, but I'm not sure if it's the memory or the music. **How Many More Years I Got?** is a two-record repackaging of three albums **(Walkin' This Road By Myself, Smokes Like Lightnin, Lightnin' and Co.)** produced by Mack McCormick for Prestige Bluesville in the early 1960s. Each places Lightnin' in a band context that is ragged but right, with Houston cronies Spider Kilpatrick on drums, Buster Pickens on piano, and Lightnin' himself on electric guitar. Along with a fourth Prestige album, **Blues in My Bottle,** a solo session that McCormick also produced, these represent to my mind the best of Lightnin's rediscovered work. This is probably because McCormick, Lightnin's long-time friend and a distinguished folklorist, knew his man well enough (read the liner notes for as unblinking and incisive a portrait of The Bluesman as you are likely to find) to keep him from coasting or offering the mechnical renditions that dominated his recorded work all through the 1960s. I would have liked this Fantasy reissue better if it had stuck more to **Walkin'** and **Smokes** and skirted **Lightnin' and Co.,** which is the weakest of the three and is here preserved intact. Ideally some of the solo session might have been thrown in, but, even flawed, this reissue is well worth seeking out both for the music and the way in which it invokes how Lightnin' must have sounded in the smoky little joints around Houston in the 1950s, 1960s, and very likely to this day.

Lowell Fulson
■ **Lowell Fulson (Arhoolie)**

The best from a long and distinguished career. The nine tracks with just his brother and himself playing guitars are achingly, almost heartbreakingly sinuous; his voice, effortlessly malleable but whipcord strong, wraps itself around a lyric with much the same effect, vocal and emotional, as George Jones achieves in country music, extracting every last ounce of feeling from a seemingly common sentiment. The band tracks, which feature Lloyd Glenn on piano and Earl Brown on alto sax, are exemplary in their way and represent the best of the Texas-California transplant.

—— TEXAS SLIDE AND ROCK 'N' ROLL ——

Frankie Lee Sims
■ **Lucy Mae Blues (Specialty)**

A great genre piece. Sims had one hit, "Lucy Mae Blues," in 1953, when he was forty-seven years old, but he got to redo it again and again and even claimed to have appeared on American Bandstand, while working with Jimmy McCracklin. Out of the same school as Lightnin' Hopkins, and sounding very much like Lightnin' at times, Sims was not as accomplished a guitarist as Hopkins, but he was a lot more percussive—and a lot louder, too—often rushing his numbers to a breathless finish in the great Texas tradition. With a strong beat, heavy amplifications, and rough gritty vocals to set off the traditional lyrics, Frankie Lee Sims can be seen as a cheerful harbinger of the new age of rock'n'roll.

L.C. Robinson
- **House Cleaning Blues (Blues on Blues)**
- **Ups and Downs (Arhoolie)**

L.C.'s nickname was "Good Rockin'," and from the evidence of these albums it's not hard to figure out why. L.C. sawed away capably on fiddle and played guitar in a style midway between Lightnin' Hopkins and Gatemouth Brown, but his specialty was steel guitar (which he learned from Bob Wills's steel player, Leon McAuliffe), an instrument practically unheard—and unheard of—in the blues. Just as Clifton Chenier transformed the accordion into a soulful instrument, Robinson got his own sound out of the steel guitar, making it an unmistakable vehicle for the blues. Sometimes he sounded like Elmore James, more often he retained the sound of his native Texas (Robinson was born in Brenham in 1915, though he settled in Oakland, California in the early 1950s).

DETROIT BLUES
ANTHOLOGY
- **Detroit Blues (Blues Classics)**

In part this amounts to a tribute to Baby Boy Warren, a native of Memphis, whose four sides with Sonny Boy Williamson (Rice Miller) dominate Side 1. In greater part this is the legacy of Hastings Street, the locus of joints and bars and loud boogie music that inspired John Lee Hooker's "Boogie Chillen." Hooker, Big Maceo, Bobo Jenkins, and Eddie Kirkland are all here, the stars of the downhome Detroit sound who, if there had been a Detroit recording industry prior to the advent of Motown, might have been as luminous as Muddy Waters, Howlin' Wolf, and Jimmy Reed seem in retrospect today. This album includes some of the best sides to have come out of Detroit's many one-shot record operations, and is a direct continuation of the Mississippi downhome tradition as it veered off to the West.

INDIVIDUAL PERFORMERS
John Lee Hooker
- **No Friend Around (Red Lightnin' or Charly)**
- **Moanin' and Stompin' the Blues (King)**
- **John Lee Hooker Alone (Specialty)**
- **Goin' Down Highway 51 (Specialty)**
- **The Blues (United) or The Greatest Hits of John Lee Hooker (United)**
- **This is Hip (Charly)**

The one Detroit superstar and, with Lightnin' Hopkins and Muddy Waters, one of the trio of downhome stars who turned blues recording around after World War II. The first five albums listed here are from Hooker's earliest period, cut between 1948 and 1952, when Hooker was at his brooding, chanting, storming best. The King and Red Lightnin' albums are as bizarre as anything that's ever come along, with titles like "Black Man Blues," "Nightmare Blues," and the suggestive "Goin' Mad Blues." There is a fury in these recordings that would never reappear in Hooker's later work; there is none of the artistry of Robert Johnson but much of the same sense of being possessed. The Specialty and UA albums are from the archives of Bernie Besman, the Detroit record store operator who essentially discovered Hooker. Although for the most part they are not the commercial recordings that were actually issued at this time, they present alternate takes and alternate titles that are just as good, and far more systematic, than those done by United, the successor to Modern (Hooker's principal label of the period). Even so, United's **The Blues** and **The Greatest Hits of John Lee Hooker** are all worth checking out (one or the other) for the original versions of the original hits. **This is Hip** is a good, varied collection of some of the best of Hooker's Vee Jay sides. Not as fierce, not as crazy as the earlier stuff, and with various bands that never quite catch on to Hooker's rhythmic and vocal idiosyncrasies, the Vee Jay sides are nonetheless worth a listen, both for their musical accessibility (not all of the solo sides possess this quality) and their delineation of an evolving style. One proviso: John Lee Hooker's music is *hard* listening and it's not particularly varied, either. In other words, don't expect to plop four or five John Lee Hooker records down on the turntable and settle in for a relaxed evening: you'll go crazy first.

—— MEMPHIS BLUES AGAIN ——

—— ANTHOLOGIES ——

- **Memphis Blues (United)**
- **Memphis and the Delta—1950s (Blues Classics)**
- **The Blues Came Down From Memphis (Charly)**
- **Union Avenue Breakdown (Charly)**
- **The Sun Box (Charly: three-record set)**

The full spectrum of postwar Memphis country blues. **Memphis Blues** includes Howlin' Wolf, Walter Horton, Bobby Bland, and Junior Parker on some of their earliest and most seminal sides. The music is crude, raw, overamplified, and frequently inaccurate—but it's wonderful to listen to and still possesses a spirit undimmed by time. **Memphis and the Delta—1950s** is a more countrified version of what was going on, with the Robert Johnson tradition well represented and taken into the electronic age by Elmore James and Boyd Gilmore and great sides from Sunnyland Slim, Roosevelt Sykes, and the white medicine-show entertainer Harmonica Frank, as well. **The Blues Came Down From Memphis,** on the other hand, is made up exclusively of Sun sides recorded by Sam Phillips between 1951 and 1954, and includes such artists as James Cotton, Rufus Thomas, and Little Milton, each of whom would one day be famous in another, altogether different guise. **Union Avenue Breakdown** is more of the same—from performers who are on the whole less well known but no less accomplished or passionate about their accomplishment. Walter Horton and Willie Nix are the standouts here. Finally **The Sun Box,** a three-record set on Charly, includes not only these representative country boogies and blues on its first record, it also features such jump blues take-offs and precursors of rock 'n' roll as "Rocket 88" by Jackie Brenston With the Delta Cats and "Mystery Train" by Little Junior's Blues Flames.

─── **INDIVIDUAL PERFORMERS** ───

Junior Parker and Bobby Bland

▪ Junior Parker and Billy Love (Charly)

One side by each artist. Billy "Red" Love is pretty forgettable. The Parker is magnificent, even if a couple of melodic themes are repeated several times. Great Memphis music, raw and progressive at the same time, with the searing guitar of Floyd Murphy or Pat Hare (later to join Muddy Waters's band) taking the lead and Little Junior's smooth, insinuating, almost plaintive voice coaxing a range of moods and emotions out of each song.

▪ Blues Consolidated—Little Junior Parker and Bobby "Blue" Bland (Duke)

Some of Parker's and Bland's earliest sides for Duke, the Houston company that took over their contract in 1954. The sound is much the same—the musicians are all out of Memphis—and Parker, who was a fine harmonica player, blows harp on record for the first time. The styles of Parker and Bland are still in embryo here, as on the **Memphis Blues** album listed above. Bland is still straining for the Roy Brown sound; he is at best a solid, if undistinguished, stand-up bluesman at this stage in time. Parker, on the other hand, has already hit upon the formula that, in its maturity, will make him one of the subtlest and most commanding blues vocalists around. For Bland's similar evolution, check out his great early albums on Duke.

B.B. King

▪ B.B. King: 1949–1950 (United)

The best-known and most illustrious of all the Memphis bluesmen, B.B. King will be considered in greater detail in a later chapter. These are his earliest sides, cut while he was still a DJ on WDIA and, as with Bobby Bland, it is obvious he is still groping for a style. There are traces of T-Bone Walker here, traces of Louis Jordan, but mostly the vocals are pure Roy Brown, in a crying falsetto that B.B. would soon adapt to his own ends.

Joe Hill Louis

▪ The One Man Band (Muskadine)

A Memphis institution, Louis played guitar, harmonica, hi-hat, and traps, often all at the same time, entertained at white folks' parties, and had his own show on WDIA as the Pepticon Boy. He was persistent about recording, appearing on a number of small Memphis labels, and had his own raw sound both on slow blues and on boogie numbers like "A Jumpin' and A Shufflin'," which are a direct link between the sophisticated jump tunes of T-Bone Walker and the "Reelin' and Rockin'" of Chuck Berry. This is not the most distinguished blues, and Louis is not the most accomplished blues player—but there's always lots of fun and, on a few numbers, evidence of deep blues feeling.

Doctor Ross

▪ Doctor Ross: His First Recordings (Arhoolie)

Another one-man band, although this time limited to harmonica and guitar. There is one dominant mood on this record, and that is: Boogie! There is a good deal of influence by John Lee Hooker, and some from Sonny Boy Williamson, too, but Isaiah Ross at his best is an exuberant, yelping, indefatigable original.

Sonny Boy Williamson (Rice Miller)
- **King Biscuit Time (Arhoolie)**

The second Sonny Boy Williamson's first recorded sides for the Jackson, Mississippi Trumpet label in 1951. The songs are classic original compositions, the accompaniment is as convincingly raw as any Memphis boogie band, and Sonny Boy, the Wizard of the Blues Harp, sings and plays as cunningly, as eloquently, as astringently as he ever would in a career that lasted until his death in 1965 and saw him achieve national recognition with the Chess label in Chicago. An essential recording from a primarily non-Memphis performer whose music can be taken as the quintessential representation of the Memphis experience.

Howlin' Wolf
- **Howlin' Wolf (Charly)**
- **Sam's Blues (Charly)**
- **Big City Blues (United)**
- **More Real Folk Blues (Chess)**

One of my very favorite singers, the man Sam Phillips called the most *unique* musician he ever met, in his Memphis period. These sides differ quite a bit from his later Chess recordings, though Wolf differed not at all. In one sense they are less focused, less menacing, more diffuse. The band is attempting to play the more progressive sounds, Wolf is singing with undiminished force, and Sam Phillips is attempting to capture both the rawness and the reality, the "badness" that he cited as the source of Howlin' Wolf's power. There is always something of a mismatch going on, but these sides—which are pretty much interchangeable—are endlessly fascinating, endlessly intriguing, endlessly delightful. Add Howlin' Wolf to Charley Patton, Robert Johnson, Muddy Waters on your list of absolutely essential recordings, and see the next chapter for a listing of his equally significant Chicago work.

12

Sweet Home Chicago

Contemporary Chicago blues starts, and in some ways may very well end, with Muddy Waters. Not only is his stylistic influence obvious on everyone from Chuck Berry to the Rolling Stones (who took their name from one of his earliest hits), but his band was also a proving ground for such artists as Little Walter, Big Walter Horton, Jimmy Rogers, Muddy's "half-brother" Otis Spann, James Cotton, and Junior Wells, all eventually influential in their own right. Furthermore, Muddy developed the tight ensemble style of play that, twenty-five years later, remains characteristic of *the* Chicago blues band, with its typical line-up of twin guitars, piano, bass, drums, harmonica, and/or horns. His music has entered the vocabulary of nearly every contemporary musician; Muddy's hit songs ("Hoochie Coochie Man," "I Just Want to Make Love to You," "Long Distance Call") have become the standards of an era.

Muddy Waters, then, unquestionably deserves all the honorifics that have been bestowed upon him: Father, Godfather, King of the Chicago Blues. But, like other attempts to pin historical evolution on a single source, this is, of course, oversimplification. Muddy Waters was, after all, a slide guitarist out of Mississippi whose chief stylistic influences were Son House and Robert Johnson. While it might be stretching a point to say that the Chicago blues was the Mississippi blues electrified, it is certainly no exaggeration to see postwar Chicago blues as a return to roots, as country blues updated, with many of its identifying characteristics and much of its standard repertoire ("Sweet Home Chicago," "Dust My Broom," "Walking Blues," even "Rolling Stone," which is itself an adaptation of the venerable "Catfish Blues") directly transplanted from Robert Johnson and Mississippi.

Postwar Chicago possessed, in any case, a unique ambience. Like Los Angeles, it was swollen by the arrival of hundreds of thousands of migrants from the South. Unlike Los Angeles, though, with its sprawling urban ghetto, the packed South Side broke down into blocks and neighborhoods that still reflected the small-town Mississippi atmosphere and parochialism, musical and social, from which many of these new residents had come. Each of these neighborhoods had its own distinct flavor, each its own music. "It used to be," Muddy Waters reminisced of his heyday in the early 1950s, "you could go down the street, just within a few blocks you'd run into four, five clubs. You could find any type of music you'd want just within the space of a few blocks." Chicago had been a recording center, too, for many years, so that when Columbia and RCA let go of their race recording series, it was only natural that someone should come along to pick up the slack.

Chess Records

That someone turned out to be two brothers: Leonard and Phil Chess. Born in Poland at about the same time as most of their major artists (Leonard was born in 1917), they immigrated to this country as children and began operating a series of bars on the South Side in 1938. An interest in music arose naturally out of their bar business, and they booked quite a bit of jazz talent along the lines of Gene Ammons or even Billie Holiday. It wasn't until after World War II, though, when the void in recording activities became apparent, that they even thought about recording. A "Hollywood agent" came in to their bar, the Macamba Lounge, to listen to a singer named Andrew Tibbs. "So I thought," said Leonard, "if he's good enough for Hollywood, I'll put him on record myself." That is what he did, and though Andrew Tibbs did not exactly claim a large place for himself in blues history, that is what got the Chess brothers involved in blues recording.

Muddy Waters came to them through Sunnyland Slim. How Sunnyland Slim came to them is not known exactly (probably the fact that he had already recorded weighed heavily, and Sunnyland has always been a good hustler), but an obvious source for much of the new recording talent in those days was not so much the clubs—which booked established acts—as the streets. On weekends the Maxwell Street open-air market was teeming with talent. Not only could you buy or barter for anything under the sun, you could hear all the latest sounds and all the old-time styles for free, as amplifier cords dangled out of second-story windows and local merchants rented out electric outlets. "Mostly every musician in Chicago played on Maxwell street at one time," said Robert Nighthawk, one of the most prominent graduates. "Including Muddy Waters. Back in the '40s, why there be one band here, one across the street, and the one that had the best music had the most people. Lots of competition. Wherever was the best band, that's where you find the people at." That's probably where you found the record companies at, too—or at least it was the source for much of their talent hunting—as little companies like Tempo Tone, Parkway, and Ora Nelle (which grew out of Maxwell Street Radio) all arose. Chess was the one to emerge out of the pack.

There is no question that Chess over the years had virtually the same impact as Sam Phillips on the course of American music. From their groping beginnings with Muddy Waters through the revolutionary work of Chuck Berry and Bo Diddley, the Chess brothers saw nearly every Chicago bluesman of any significance pass

*Muddy Waters's band set the standard for tight ensemble work
that became the trademark of the Chicago blues sound.*
Courtesy of Chess Records/*Living Blues*

through their studio at one time or another and, like Phillips, they
developed pragmatic recording techniques (homemade echo and a
primative system of tape delay) that perfectly captured the music
they were helping to evolve. Nonetheless, it seems obvious that they
were not quite sure what they had at first. From the beginning, when
the success of Muddy Waters's "Can't Be Satisfied" took them by
surprise, through their subsequent reluctance to allow Waters to
bring his working band into the studio, right up to their formation of
the newly named Chess label in 1950, they were more or less groping for a style. Even with the establishment of the Chess imprint, their
first release was Gene Ammons's hit instrumental "My Foolish
Heart." Their second—and the record that finally established them
on a firm blues course—was Muddy Waters's "Rollin' Stone."

Muddy Waters

If Chess had till then been unsure of what to do with him, Muddy
Waters never seems to have had a moment's doubt. Born McKinley
Morganfield in Rolling Fork, Mississippi, in 1915, he was brought up
in Clarksdale and raised in the classic Delta tradition. It seems
scarcely coincidental that he should have been first discovered in
Stovall, Mississippi, in 1941, when folklorist Alan Lomax was researching the Robert Johnson tradition. Nor does it seem even remotely accidental that Muddy Waters should have gone on to record
professionally and make commercial blues records. For when he left
Mississippi in 1943, he fully intended, unlike many of his contemporaries, to be a professional musician. In 1947 he got a session for
Columbia with Lester Melrose (oddly enough, Johnny Shines was recorded at virtually the same time in much the same style) and,
though the sides were never released commercially, within a year he
had made his first records for Leonard Chess. He was not the first of
the new Chicago blues singers to record nor, it turned out, did the
records reflect his full ensemble sound at first but, like Lightnin'
Hopkins and John Lee Hooker, he exploded on the downhome

rhythm and blues scene when his first single on the newly formed Chess label hit the charts in 1950. Within a short time he was able to bring his full band into the studio, a band that consisted at that point of the remarkable harmonica virtuoso, Little Walter, Muddy's "half-brother" Otis Spann on piano, the intricate interplay of Waters's and Jimmy Rogers's two guitars breathing as a single voice, and the solid rhythm section of Big Crawford and Elgin Evans on bass and drums. There had never been a blues band quite like this before, with so solid an ensemble sound, and as Muddy had more and more hits the music became more and more insistent, achieving what Leonard Chess believed sold records: "Drums, drums, and more drums." By the time he achieved his popular peak, Muddy Waters had become a shouting, declamatory kind of singer who had for-saken his guitar as a kind of anachronism and whose band played with a single pulsating rhythm. It was only after his records stopped selling in the rhythm and blues market that he took up guitar again and only in the latter stages of his career, when he had been redis-covered as a kind of "folk singer," that he went back to the Missis-sippi repertoire for which he was originally famous. In the meantime, a whole generation of singers had adopted his tight ensemble ap-proach, bluesmen like Floyd Jones, J.B. Hutto, Arthur "Big Boy" Spires, Eddie Taylor, all of whom aspired to the Muddy Waters sound, which to a lesser extent was the basis for Bo Diddley's and Chuck Berry's rock 'n' roll novelties.

Elmore James

Other elements from the same tradition—as significant artistically if not commercially—continued to develop at the same time. Elmore James, a contemporary of Muddy Waters who was equally influ-enced by Robert Johnson, made something of a career out of what may be Johnson's best-known song, "Dust My Broom," which James first recorded in 1951, at the age of thirty-two, with Sonny Boy Williamson II (Rice Miller), another Johnson compatriot, on harmon-ica. In James's versions of this and other songs from the Johnson canon, the music takes on an almost hysterical edge, as high frantic vocals—constantly on the verge of breaking up—combine with slashing slide guitar to provide a veneer of emotionalism that is ab-sent from the work of Muddy Waters. It was this frenetic edge that most distinguished Elmore James, and indeed some of his later work, which fuses the country-blues style of Robert Johnson with soul riffs of the 1960s ("The Sky is Crying," "Something Inside of Me"), is among the most affecting of modern blues styles. Perhaps because he did not record primarily for Chess, or perhaps because his style was so unrelievedly intense, James never achieved the commercial popularity of Muddy Waters, but he was widely popular in Chicago and throughout the South and continued to record exten-sively for a dozen years until his death.

Robert Nighthawk

Robert Nighthawk, too, played in the Mississippi bottleneck tradi-tion, though he was born in Helena, Arkansas, in 1909. Something of an influence on Elmore James and Muddy Waters (he played at Muddy's first wedding in 1932, where the festivities got so uproarious that the two-room plantation shack tumbled down), he first recorded with Big Joe Williams and the first Sonny Boy Williamson in a historic 1937 session, just a year after Robert Johnson, also Nighthawk's junior, made his first recordings. His style did not fully form, though, until the 1940s, when he is said to have been among the first bluesmen to amplify his guitar and adapt the fluid bottleneck style of Tampa Red to the postwar sound. Nighthawk's blues were, in fact, a singular mix, combining unquestionable urbanity with the deep feeling of the downhome blues, reflecting not only the sound of the Delta but the more sophisticated influences of Lonnie Johnson, Tampa Red, and Leroy Carr as well. He sang in a deep crooning voice, and his slide playing was as smooth and creamy as that of his mentor, Tampa Red. Significantly, it was Muddy Waters who brought him in to the Chess studio where, in 1949, he recorded as Robert Nighthawk for the first time (in the prewar years, he had been Robert Lee McCoy, Rambling Bob, and Peetie's Boy, though his real name was Robert Lee McCollum). That initial record, "Sweet Black Angel," backed by "Annie Lee," was a double-sided hit, predating even Muddy's "Rollin' Stone." Both tunes were originally recorded by Tampa Red and remained Nighthawk's signature pieces even after B.B. King had made a far bigger hit with his 1956 variation, "Sweet Little Angel." They also marked the entrance into the Chess studio of Willie Dixon, a portly bass player who had previously recorded for Lester Melrose and who in a sense became the Lester Melrose of the new era, but with an added distinction: not only did he produce, set up sessions, and talent scout for Chess and other labels, he wrote many of the Chess blues stable's biggest hits as well. For some reason, Nighthawk did not continue long with Chess, and his subsequent recording career was sporadic and unsuccessful, punctuated by frequent returns to the South and ending up on Maxwell Street, where he and Muddy Waters and just about everyone else had started out.

Robert Jr. Lockwood

Another equally interesting, if less characteristic, career is that of Robert Jr. Lockwood, Robert Johnson's stepson. Lockwood was christened after his father but became known as Robert Jr. throughout his adult life because of his association with the famous bluesman, actually only four years his senior. Born in 1915 in Marvell, Arkansas, not far from Helena, Lockwood made his first guitar from a record player with the help of his celebrated stepfather and, when Johnson died, gave up playing for a while "because I didn't know nothing but his songs." When he first recorded in 1941, it was with four classic sides in the Johnson tradition (actually two may have been written—though they were never recorded—by Johnson). He also began playing with Sonny Boy Williamson II on the radio around this time, and it was perhaps in this way that he got into the more progressive jazz-influenced sounds that characterize his mature work and with which he heavily influenced B.B. King during his years in Memphis in the late 1940s. After moving to Chicago around 1950, he became one of the stalwart Chess house musicians, backing everyone from the Moonglows to Muddy Waters, Little Walter, and Chuck Berry, providing the faultless rhythm patterns and jaunty, jazzy fills that came to characterize the Chess sound. His own career definitely suffered because he lacked the vocal command of the great bluesmen, possessing instead a dry, somewhat nasal voice, and he recorded only sporadically under his own name over the years, never actually appearing as a solo artist for Chess. It was only after he moved to Cleveland in 1961 and was forced to front his own bands that he really came to develop a sound of his own, and he didn't record extensively until the 1970s, when specialist blues labels like Delmark, Trix, and Rounder sought him out. In his new career he has turned his back on the bottleneck style and what he calls the old "bomp-de-bomp" blues and has chosen instead to further the eclectic side— as opposed to the reverential one—of the Robert Johnson tradition. Together with Johnny Shines, whom he first got to know through Robert Johnson in the early 1930s and rejoined as a partner when both were in their sixties, he has sought to redefine our perception of Johnson, viewing him not as someone who would endlessly repeat the same riffs, style, and repertoire, but as a venturesome, stubborn, and exploratory bluesman. Much in the manner of Robert Jr. Lockwood and Johnny Shines.

Johnny Shines

Johnny Shines, of course, has become widely known as Robert Johnson's most dedicated and inventive disciple. Born in 1915 in Frazier, Tennessee, Shines seems closest to Johnson both in his style and in his extraordinarily fertile creative imagination. He met Robert Johnson in 1935 in Helena and traveled with him off and on for the next two or three years. Shines moved to Chicago in 1941 (hoping eventually to get to Africa), and had an unreleased session for Columbia in 1946, a few months before Muddy Waters cut his first sides for Lester Melrose, also unissued at the time. Muddy never let this initial failure deter him for a moment, of course, but whether because he lacked Muddy's fierce determination or simply because he never joined forces effectively with Chess, Johnny Shines had little recording success from a commercial point of view from that time on. "I might have hooked up with twenty-five other companies, but I wanted to go with Chess," Johnny has said of his aborted career with the company. He made a record for them in 1950, but it was never released because, Johnny thought, there were concurrent hits by Muddy Waters, Little Walter, and Eddie Ware. When Chess finally wanted to release it, Johnny blocked the release, because he had another contract with J.O.B. by now, "but even so, the other record never was a hit, it never got played. And I believe Chess did that, too." Eventually Shines just quit the life, disgusted and disillusioned, and he didn't take it up again until the mid-1960s, when he was located by Mike Rowe, an English blues historian. Since then, like Lockwood, he has recorded frequently and fruitfully, with brilliant original compositions, lovely slide playing, and a voice as shatteringly effective as anything the blues has to offer, providing one more glimpse of directions in which the Robert Johnson tradition might have gone.

Howlin' Wolf created his own music from the influences of the outstanding Mississippi bluesmen, but his performing style was uniquely his own.
Courtesy of *Living Blues*

Howlin' Wolf

Johnny Shines's two models when he was young were Robert Johnson and Howlin' Wolf. The pervasive influence of the first should be obvious by now, but Wolf's role is somewhat more problematic. Perhaps the only way to suggest its dimensions is to say that the Howlin' Wolf personified the spirit of the blues. As Sam Phillips said, there was no one like him before or since; although his music was classic, no one sang like Howlin' Wolf, and while he clearly sprang from the tradition of Charley Patton and Tommy Johnson (and Son House and Robert Johnson, whom he also knew as a young man) he was just as clearly *sui generis*. After he came to Chicago, his music changed a little. His bands became tighter and perhaps in the process a little less adventurous. He experimented with horns, moved away from the boogie music of Memphis, and established a characteristic slow-rocking groove. Unlike Muddy Waters's, though, his style did not particularly evolve. No matter who was in his band, no matter how outstanding the individual musicians, the focus was always Wolf, and *he* was always Wolf, singing, talking, playing, in that inimitable style, growling in that hoarse rasp that could be mistaken for no one else, alternating a fierce attack with a surprising delicacy of phrasing and dynamics. His music always stemmed from just what he was feeling, and you can hear the shifts in mood even on record, improvisations (emotional, not musical), on a moment's notice. He was a strange mix of qualities, sensitive and suspicious, menacing and vulnerable at the same time, driven to compete with every other blues singer that he encountered; so much so that when at sixty-five, with a bad heart, and on dialysis treatment he found himself on stage with B.B. King, Bobby Bland, and Little Milton, just two months before his death, it was Wolf who was crawling around the stage, hurling his huge bulk around, putting out every ounce of energy he possessed, trying to win the plaudits of the crowd. And he did. Although there was no school of Wolf (there couldn't have been), there was no doubt in Chicago that he was chief claimant to Muddy's throne, a claim he put forth again and again on stage and in interviews, making no bones of the rivalry and declaring on the one occasion when they met on record, "I'm the king, I'm the king, I done tole you all, I'm the king of the blues."

Sonny Boy Williamson II

Although he prided himself on his guitar playing, which was indifferent at best, Howlin' Wolf's first instrument was the harmonica, and his first teacher, back in Mississippi when they were brothers-in-law, was the second Sonny Boy Williamson. Like Wolf one of the primary exponents of the rough jump blues of Memphis and a blues personality known all throughout the South, Sonny Boy moved to Chicago later than most, in the mid-1950s, after stays in Detroit and Milwaukee. In fact he never really gave up Helena as his home and continued traveling all over the South right up until his death, but it was in Chicago that he became a star, recording, like Muddy and Wolf, for Chess and playing a big part in helping to put blues harmonica on a level with blues guitar, not just as another instrument but as one of the lead voices in a Chicago blues band.

Born around the turn of the century in Glendora, Mississippi, Sonny Boy, according to Johnny Shines, used to travel quite a lot by himself, walking and playing his harp from "coast to coast. He'd been quite exposed to the public not in the real show in the limelight but I mean house-to-house exposure." He had also played and traveled with Robert Johnson, Robert Nighthawk, Elmore James, Robert Jr. Lockwood, and Shines himself, and when he first came to record for the Jackson, Mississippi-based Trumpet label in 1951, had already been a star on radio for ten years. When he finally came to Chicago, he was an older man, closer in style to the country blues of the 1920s and 1930s than some of his Chess compatriots, but at the same time more witty, more original, and more striking as a writer, singer and instrumentalist than many of the modernists whose work today seems brittle and derivative. Sonny Boy Williamson projected a Mephistophelian persona and carried it out in his songs. The thin astringent tone of his harmonica, the sensitivity of his phrasing, his impeccable timing are all immediately recognizable and were absorbed by such diverse students as Junior Wells, James Cotton, Little Junior Parker, and Wolf himself. He was not incapable of harmonica pyrotechnics either, but it is the sly originality of his lyrics, the forceful allusiveness of his singing, the uniqueness of his compositions that set him off from other harp players and establish him as one of the great bluesmen of his time, one whose deceptive straightforwardness only conceals a deeper meaning. He had a great influence on a whole generation of English rock groups—the Animals, the Yardbirds, the Rolling Stones—whom he met and played with on European tours in 1964 and 1965, but when he died back in Helena in 1965, Paul Oliver writes, "He was working the joints and still playing on the King Biscuit Show as he had a quarter of a century before. Hardly anyone believed his story that he had been touring European concert halls," though with his "two-tone harlequin suit in black and charcoal gray made in an English tailor's and with rolled umbrella, bowler, and kid gloves," it must have seemed obvious that he had traveled further than Fort Smith, Arkansas.

The two other Chicago harmonica stars to reckon with were Little Walter and Big Walter. In the hands of the first Sonny Boy Williamson, blues harmonica had taken on a new cachet, as Sonny Boy I became the first harmonica star. Sonny Boy II, on the other hand, contributed a number of unforgettable songs and strongly influenced the Memphis blues and the blues of the South through his radio shows and recordings. Both Little Walter Jacobs and Big Walter Horton were instrumental virtuosos, raising blues harmonica playing to new heights and creating a new role and a new standard for this once-lowly instrument.

Walter Horton

Walter Horton was the older man, born in Horn Lake, Mississippi, in 1918, and an early acquaintance of Johnny Shines and Robert Johnson. "I met Walter, really, in 1930," Shines has said, "and he would be sitting on the porch, blowing in tin cans, you know, and he'd get sounds out of those things." A key figure on the postwar Memphis blues scene, Horton recorded extensively for Sam Phillips and eventually moved to Chicago to join the Muddy Waters band as a replacement for Little Walter. Never much of a vocalist, Horton was known on record both as "Mumbles" and "Shakey Walter," perhaps in recognition of his erratic singing, but his harmonica playing, both on his own records and in his uncompromisingly lyrical solos on just about everyone else's (he stands out on sides by Muddy, Johnny Shines, and Jimmy Rogers in particular) is breathtaking. In a sense, he embodies the classic definition of a musician's musician, an artist universally recognized by his peers who has had an enormous impact on musicians who are much better known, including his namesake, Little Walter.

Little Walter

Little Walter, of course, is the one figure who is always cited as the paramount example of blues harp playing. He emerged from the Muddy Waters band at the age of twenty-two in 1952 with what may have been the biggest postwar country-blues hit, an instrumental that the band had been using as a set opener and closer, originally entitled "Your Cat Will Play" and renamed "Juke" by Leonard Chess. When the record came out, the band was in Louisiana. "He heard that record on the radio," pianist Otis Spann recalled shortly before his death, "next thing you look up and Walter was gone."

Over the course of the next half dozen years, Little Walter virtually revolutionized blues harmonica by harnessing technology to feeling and coming up with what seemed like a whole new sound. On his earliest records for Ora Nelle and Parkway in the late 1940s, he sounds very much like the first Sonny Boy Williamson, whom he was obviously emulating, but by the time he got to Chess he had amplified his instrument (Walter Horton, too, blew shattering amplified harp) and combined technological innovation with a ceaseless flow of ideas, a sweeping saxophonelike tone, sure-handed execution, and a sledgehammer attack to produce some of the most emotion-

The rivalry between Howlin' Wolf and Muddy Waters was legendary;
Wolf was the chief claimant to Muddy's throne.
Courtesy of Tom Copi

ally charged blues instrumentals of the postwar years. He was an enormously popular artist, actually outstripping in sales both his mentor, Muddy Waters, and the Howlin' Wolf, and his light, not particularly forceful voice, and familiar pastiches of blues lyrics seemed to appeal to a broader market than the hard blues of Muddy and Wolf. When he died in 1968, he was still a young man, but he had lost his assurance and his instrumental chops and scarcely recorded at all in the last five years of his life.

Otis Spann

The chief piano player on the postwar Chicago blues scene came out of the Muddy Waters band as well. In fact, Otis Spann, who died in 1970 at the age of forty, was one of the few blues piano players who could also take his place in the ranks of great blues singers. Following in the path of Big Maceo, his stylistic mentor, Spann, according to Muddy Waters, had "that *bad* left hand, both hands bad. If you playing the blues, the man can play with you. He don't care what kind of time you break, he can break it with you. There's a man who was raised singing the blues, he was raised in Mississippi, and he *knows* the blues." As great as were his pianistic skills (and Spann could handle everything from rollicking rock'n'roll to the most brooding, somber blues), his crowning glory was his voice. Curiously enough, here, too, he emulated Maceo, singing in warm, hoarse, slightly boozy tones and conveying a melancholy warmth, a movingly personal charm. Like Maceo, Spann was the most intimate of blues singers, and while he may never have achieved the heights of a major bluesman like Muddy Waters, his blues were always sincere and movingly personal, and his piano playing bridged the gap between boogie woogie and the dark rolling sound of the Mississippi blues.

Sunnyland Slim

One other pianist who is often overlooked but deserves mention is Sunnyland Slim, a ubiquitous figure who started recording in 1944 as Doctor Clayton's Buddy and was among the first of the Chicago bluesmen to record in the new postwar style. Sunnyland introduced Muddy Waters to the recording studio, made innumerable records with Muddy, Memphis Minnie, Howlin' Wolf, and just about every other significant figure on the Chicago blues scene, and has continued to cut records into the 1980s that, while too often rehashes of Sunnyland Slim standards, are sometimes raw slices of the blues. Johnny Shines said of him, "Sunnyland was in the honky tonk business, and people knew him as a honky tonk player. Maybe he wouldn't say it himself, or maybe he wouldn't like the idea of me saying it, but there's nothing else you can say." His personality has never lent itself to easy adoption, and his music is not as striking or as personal as Otis Spann's but Sunnyland Slim has been a mainstay of the Chicago blues scene for nearly forty years and remains one of the most distinctive accompanists with the deep blues sound who is still around.

Jimmy Rogers

Finally, to expand upon the Muddy Waters and Chess connections, there is Jimmy Rogers, the second guitarist in Muddy's first great band, whose almost instinctive responses to Muddy's dramatic slide-guitar lead formed an intricate pattern of counterpoint and rhythm that was as much at the heart of the Muddy Waters sound as Otis Spann's piano or Little Walter's harmonica. Rogers, born James A. Lane in Mississippi in 1926, had a recording career of his own, not as commercially successful as Little Walter's but with its share of hits nonetheless. He would generally record at the end of a Muddy Waters session, using the same band and thus further perpetuating the same sound that had defined the Chicago blues. Although he had nowhere near as forceful a voice or presence as Waters, he possessed an easygoing, relaxed style that showed off the band sound to perfection. His numbers became a vehicle, in a sense, for the ensemble style, a jumping-off point for some of Little Walter's and Big Walter's and Otis Spann's most imaginative solos. His signature tune, "That's All Right," an adaptation of a Robert Jr. Lockwood song first recorded as "Ora Nelle Blues" by Othum Brown before Muddy Waters ever recorded for Leonard Chess, became one of the theme songs of the Chicago blues, a part of everyone's standard repertoire. When Rogers quit playing with Muddy in 1959, there was a void in the Muddy Waters band that was never filled, and though Muddy tried hard with two, and sometimes three, additional guitars to fill out the sound, he never found anyone to complement him so sympathetically or to form so ideal an unspoken partnership.

Jimmy Reed

One last note on the commercial Chicago blues—and perhaps an apology is in order here as well for leaving till now any mention of the most commercially successful and most widely influential Chicago blues singer of all, Jimmy Reed. Like Muddy, Wolf, Sonny Boy, Reed was born in Mississippi, in Dunleith in 1925, but his sound was a little different from that of any of the hard blues singers, being based on his own crudely strummed guitar and rack harmonica, a walking bass that was supplied by his boyhood friend Eddie Taylor on second guitar, and vocals so loose that they have often been called mush-mouthed. His blues did not possess any of the emotional thrust of Muddy's or Wolf's, nor did they suggest anything like the instrumental virtuosity or adventuresomeness of Little Walter or Robert Jr. Lockwood. Instead, they were simple, easily imitated, repetitive melodies and collages of stock lyrics, accessible to whites as well as blacks, in a way that deep Delta blues have never been. Perhaps his role can best be compared to that of a popularizer like Tampa Red or even Bumble Bee Slim, another indifferent instrumentalist who was enormously popular in the 1930s. From 1955 to 1966 Jimmy Reed had fourteen Top Forty rhythm and blues hits, more than any other blues singer except B.B. King; twelve of them crossed over onto the pop charts as well, something almost unheard of for any black artist, let alone a bluesman. He recorded for Vee Jay, a black-owned Chicago label that alone rivaled Chess and, with Chess, was the only blues label to cross over into soul production to any extent. (Vee Jay, for a brief moment, also had the American rights to the Beatles at the beginning of their career.) So Reed's career should dispel a couple of myths set up in this chapter: the uncontested hegemony of Chess and the invariable parochialism of the blues audience. Reed remained enormously popular on the white fraternity circuit right up until his death in 1976, and his records have continued to sell. His lazy slurred sound left its mark on a whole generation of black singers and also provided the inspiration, and the example, that allowed far more emotive white blues singers like Charlie Rich, Elvis Presley, and Lonnie Mack to try the blues themselves.

Chicago blues of the classic variety is still going on. New voices, new compositions are still being added, and the standard repertoire has not even begun to turn stale. Muddy Waters is more famous today than he could ever have imagined possible even in his heyday; he has made triumphant tours of Europe, headlined rock concerts, and been universally hailed as "The Father of the Blues." But Muddy Waters never had another rhythm and blues hit after 1958. Little Walter's last big hit, a tasteful version of Big Bill Broonzy's "Key to the Highway," came in the same year. What had happened by then was that rock and roll and contemporary rhythm and blues had replaced downhome blues as the popular black music of the day. Rock'n'roll provided the vehicle for the entrance of younger blues-oriented musicians into the world of popular music. Chess itself turned to slicker sounds, though the label never stopped recording Muddy, Wolf, Little Walter, and Sonny Boy Williamson as long as Leonard Chess and the individual artists were still alive. And those black people who were still listening to the blues—not an inconsiderable number by any means—were buying the up-to-date sounds put down by B.B. King and inspired by T-Bone Walker, a sleek new brand of blues that left the hamlets of Mississippi far behind.

SELECTED RECORDINGS

— ANTHOLOGIES —

■ **Chicago Blues: The Beginning (Testament)**
  Includes the Johnny Shines/Muddy Waters recordings made for

Lester Melrose in 1946 but unissued until 1971. Fascinating glimpses of the Chicago style in embryo. Muddy doesn't play slide; Shines is recording acoustic blues in standard tuning. With both, the Robert Johnson influence comes through strongly, and on the Muddy Waters cuts you can hear the beginnings of the modern band style, with Sunnyland Slim on piano, an unidentified rhythm section, and the hard-driving sound of Muddy himself. Beautiful music, and an incomparable opportunity to eavesdrop on history.

- **Chicago Blues: The Early 1950s (Blues Classics)**
- **On the Road Again (Muskadine)**
- **Take a Little Walk With Me (Boogie Disease)**

The classic Chicago Blues. No Muddy or Wolf or any of the Chess stars (except in a supporting role), but the sound, the beat, the emotion that defined the postwar Chicago style. Homesick James, pre-Chess Little Walter, Big Walter, Robert Nighthawk, J.B. Hutto, Sunnyland Slim—all drift in and out of these anthologies with some of their finest sides. Johnny Shines's earliest records for J.O.B. are here (on **On the Road Again**) with superlative support from Walter Horton on harmonica. Baby Face Leroy's *insane* two-part "Rollin' and Tumblin' " (on **Chicago Blues**) with contributory humming from Muddy Waters and Little Walter includes some of the eeriest concatenations ever laid down on record. I think if I had to choose, I would pick the first two albums as the more essential, but these are, and set, the absolute standards of an era.

- **Chicago Slickers, 1948–1953 (Nighthawk)**

Another of the Nighthawk label's invaluable addenda to history. Here are two more Johnny Shines/Walter Horton collaborations, the first appearance together on record of Little Walter and Muddy Waters (under Walter's name), some great 1948 Floyd Jones in the Muddy Waters manner (which in 1948 may have been just as much the Floyd Jones manner), and more Sunnyland Slim, Homesick James, and Robert Nighthawk. The rarest and some of the best of the postwar Chicago blues, perhaps secondary in familiarity but not in quality to the albums listed above.

- **Genesis Vols. I–III (English Chess: each a three-record set)**

Of doubtful availability, these sets go as far towards telling the story of Chess as anything else to date (or anything looming on the horizon). Not without their faults, and containing some material that would already be in the hands of the average collector, these are nonetheless as essential as any of the albums listed above. Not only do you get Muddy Waters's earliest sides (Vol. I), the whole Memphis-to-Chicago story (Vol. II, which concentrates on Sonny Boy Williamson, Robert Nighthawk, and Howlin' Wolf), and the consolidation of the Chicago sound (Jimmy Rogers, Little Walter, and Muddy's greatest hits) on Vol. III, you also get a lavishly illustrated booklet crammed with discographical, historical, and biographical information with each set. There probably could have been half a dozen more volumes like these, documenting the rise and fall of Chess, but unfortunately money and interest ran out and Chess was sold subsequent to the issuance of Vol. III, so it is doubtful if so systematic a study will soon be undertaken again.

- **Drop Down Mama (Chess, Vintage series)**

■ **Sultans of the Slide Guitar (Blues Ball)**

More Chess sides, this time concentrating—as the title of the latter anthology suggests—on the bottleneck guitar style. **Drop Down Mama** is one of the great modern blues anthologies, including not only Johnny Shines's original Chess recordings, finally issued (without permission) after twenty years, but also Robert Nighthawk's first Chess session—which produced "Sweet Black Angel" and "Anna Lee"—and more great sides from Floyd Jones and the eccentric Robert Johnson disciple, Honeyboy Edwards.

■ **Chicago/The Blues/Today! Vols. 1–3 (Vanguard)**

Produced by Sam Charters during a whirlwind tour of Chicago in 1965, these albums marked the return to record of Junior Wells, J.B. Hutto, Otis Rush, Homesick James, and Johnny Shines, among others, for a new collector market. All are still young, all still sense the possibilities for stardom here. Accompaniment is frequently ragged, bands are unrehearsed, but the very impromptu nature of the recordings stands them in good stead, as enthusiasm and spontaneity run high. Otis Spann's percussion-accompanied set on Vol. 1 is a high point; so is J.B. Hutto's emotionally charged collection of somewhat incoherent (difficult-to-understand) originals. Otis Rush sings and plays as well on Vol. 2 as he has since his sensational recording debut for Cobra in 1956, though unfortunately only one of the songs is his own. Johnny Shines's partnership with Walter Horton on Vol. 3, however, remains unquestionably the high point, and his re-creation of Robert Johnson's "Terraplane" as "Dynaflow Blues" is an emotional burst of sheer exuberance almost unequalled on record.

— **INDIVIDUAL PERFORMERS** —
— **SLIDE PLAYERS** —

Muddy Waters

■ **McKinley Morganfield A.K.A. Muddy Waters**
(Chess: two-record set)

The best of Muddy Waters, with all the familiar standards and all the biggest hits. This well-chosen selection reprograms three earlier albums into a double-record set. **The Best of Muddy Waters** (**Sail On** in a second life) is here in its entirety; **The Real Folk Blues** and **More Real Folk Blues** are here in part. See if you can find the latter, for it includes many of Waters's earliest and most strongly Robert Johnson-influenced sides, with nothing but Muddy's elegiac slide playing, Little Walter's unamplified harp, and Big Crawford's acoustic bass. These are truly echoes of another era, but **McKinley Morganfield A.K.A. Muddy Waters** brings us right up to date, with the Muddy Waters band sound predominating and the heavy beat that would soon give way to rock'n'roll.

■ **Back In the Early Days (Syndicate Chapter: two-record set)**

A British bootleg of what was left out of the Chess set mentioned above. The sound quality is only fair, and some of the later material is a little marginal, but once again the early sides (including "Feel Like Going Home," the Robert Johnson/Robert Lockwood "Mean Red Spider," and a country dance tune called "Evans Shuffle") sparkle with some of Muddy's loveliest and most deeply felt playing.

Elmore James
- **Original Folk Blues (United)**
- **The Legend of Elmore James (United)**
- **The Resurrection of Elmore James (United)**

The best of Elmore's early sides for the Bihari brothers' various labels. Wild, anarchic, hovering on the edge of total abandonment of control. There are some wonderful moments here, the soulful edge to "Goodbye Baby" **(Original Folk Blues)**, the two on-location recordings made in a Canton, Mississippi joint on **The Legend Of**, the crazy horn parts, and endless variations on the "Dust My Broom" theme. You can't go wrong with Elmore, though; like the Howlin' Wolf, he invariably gave his all, and this comes through over and over again in the emotional catharsis of his recordings. (**The Best of Elmore James**—on the English Ace label, includes a good—if not very extensive selection from these three albums.)
- **One Way Out (Charly)**
- **Got to Move (Charly)**

Equally exciting collections from his later, and arguably greater, Bobby Robinson-recorded material. If Elmore's early blues seemed emotion-laden, these almost reach the point of being overwrought. What saves them is the evident lack of calculation, the ringing clarity of Elmore's slide guitar, and the incontestable emotional involvement, which never degenerates into mere mannerism.

Robert Nighthawk
- **Bricks in My Pillow (Pearl)**
- **Live on Maxwell Street (Rounder)**
- **Robert Nighthawk-Houston Stackhouse (Testament)**

As sweetly lyric as Muddy Waters was deeply stoic or Elmore James simply manic. Nighthawk is one of the great romantic bluesmen. The Pearl album consists of the commercial sides, released and unreleased, that he made in 1951 and 1952 after his short-lived career with Chess was over. They contain some beautiful slide performances, some strongly Tommy Johnson-influenced cuts, and a number of up-to-date jump numbers, all of which show Nighthawk as a performer of remarkable consistency, execution, and taste. The Rounder album is a 1964 Maxwell Street performance, complete with incidental crowd noise and good-natured shouts of encouragement. It is a significant find, showing a major bluesman stretching out, fooling around with ideas and repertoire, casually establishing mood and ambience in a rough informal setting. The Testament album stems from the same period and coincides with Nighthawk's last extended stay in Chicago. Just a lyric as the earliest sides, and just as accomplished, this Pete Welding production offers as an added bonus four cuts by Houston Stackhouse, a great if underrated Tommy Johnson-influenced bluesman who was Nighthawk's original teacher.

Johnny Shines
- **Johnny Shines and Robert Lockwood (Flyright)**

Here are Johnny Shines's great 1952–1953 J.O.B. sides, together with Robert Lockwood's first postwar session, which included the first postwar recording of "Dust My Broom," beating Elmore James's version by a few months. Shines's sessions, much of which remained unissued until this 1980 Flyright release, contain some of the greatest postwar sides in the Robert Johnson tradition, with explosive duets with Walter Horton, brilliant slide playing, and consistently challenging lyrics. What strikes me here, as with so much of Shines's work, is the study in contrasts between the powerful vibrato and subtle dynamics of his magnificently expressive voice, between the solidly traditional grounding and the highly experimental imagination that are at work in these songs. The five Lockwood cuts on the other hand, are interesting but hardly essential.

- **Last Night's Dream (Blue Horizon)**
- **Johnny Shines (Testament)**
- **Johnny Shines with Big Walter Horton (Testament)**
- **Johnny Shines (Advent)**

The best of Shines's post-rediscovery career. On his later albums he doesn't take the trouble to retune his guitar but instead plays slide in standard tuning. Here you get the full Delta tuning, refined by a very modern sensibility. **Last Night's Dream** remains for me the most interesting for its original compositions, though apart from Shines's guitar—and even including his pieces in standard tuning—it is very much flawed musically. The first Testament album is made up of predominantly traditional material, with sparkling support from Walter Horton and Otis Spann and a fascinating and troubling "Mr. Tom Green's Farm," which relates the story of brutal treatment on a prison farm. **Johnny Shines with Big Walter Horton** seems to consist of outtakes from this and another session and is more uneven as a result, but it contains several wonderful cuts, including a great "Worried Life Blues." All the previous albums are band albums exclusively. Advent's **Johnny Shines** shows off Shines as a fairly convincing contemporary soul singer and as a solo acoustic folk artist. The band cuts have backing from Philip Walker's fine L.A.-based group. I find the acoustic work a little sterile, but this is as good a representation of this latter-day phase of Shines's career as you're going to get. If you enjoy it, try **Standing at the Crossroads** on Testament, which consists for the most part of reworkings of Robert Johnson songs.

Robert Jr. Lockwood

- **Contrasts (Trix)**
- **Does 12 (Trix)**
- **Hangin' On (Rounder)**

Contrasts is the theme. The first album contains bebop, ballads, boogie, and blues, and is about as enterprising a record as I can think of by a traditional blues singer. It's the kind of record that makes you just want to smile with pleasure, and Lockwood even allowed himself to be persuaded to do an acoustic slide version of "Little Boy Blue," something almost unthinkable for a man who refuses to look back. **Does 12** is more of the same, as Robert Jr. Lockwood discovers the twelve-string guitar (hence the punning title) and makes it sound like a celeste. More jazz, more variety, and more confident vocals from Lockwood who, up until the 1970s when these albums were recorded, had never really been much of a solo artist at all. **Hangin' On** celebrates the new-found, old-remembered partnership of Johnny Shines and Robert Lockwood. One half consists of acoustic duets, with separate vocals from Shines and Lockwood and a churning instrumental called "Razzmadazz." For me, the most interesting parts of the album, though, are Lockwood's ventures into funk on tunes like "Hangin' On" and "Here It Is, Brother," wherein Robert describes his anticipated debut on "Soul Train." Try the Trix first, but this is fun, too, if somewhat confounding to critics of Shines and Lockwood who would like to see them stay in the same old bag.

Johnny Littlejohn
■ **John Littlejohn's Chicago Blues Stars (Arhoolie)**

A great album by a good artist. Fine original material by Littlejohn and Willie Dixon, and the few songs with which Littlejohn is associated, totally in the Elmore James mold. Littlejohn lacks the charismatic anarchy of Elmore, and he never had much of a recording career, but oh that slide!

— MAINSTREAM MUSIC —

Jimmy Rogers
■ **Chicago Bound (Chess)**

The most obvious choice, since he has backing him *the* Chicago band. These are his best sides, every one a gem (there aren't many records you can say that about), and though there is a later double-record set called just **Jimmy Rogers** (also on Chess), it doesn't improve any on the selection here. Think of Rogers as a neutral vehicle with a pleasant voice, and what you have here is some of the finest Chicago blues on wax.

— THE ORIGINAL HOWLIN' WOLF AND HIS ORCHESTRA —

Howlin' Wolf
■ **Chester Burnett A.K.A. Howlin' Wolf (Chess: two-record set)**

The Howlin' Wolf, as should be evident by now, was a category unto himself. There is nothing more exciting, dynamic, dramatic, or enthralling in the blues. This is an album of greatest hits, made up of selections from four earlier records: **Howlin Wolf**, **Evil**, **The Real Folk Blues**, and **More Real Folk Blues** (all Chess). The last is from his Memphis period, which has already been discussed. The other performances are more polished, the Chicago bands are definitely more together, but the effect is no less spontaneous or deep. It would be impossible to imagine a blues library without this essential collection, but if you were able to find the original albums, each of them (with the possible exception of **The Real Folk Blues**, whose high points I think make up for its unevenness) is well worth having.
■ **Going Back Home (Syndicate Chapter)**

More early and middle-period sides bootlegged from Chess on this British label. The sound is definitely inferior to the official Chess issues, but the music is not. These sides are less familiar than the hits, primarily because Chess never reissued them on LP, but the effect is no less striking or hypnotic. A worthy companion volume to the Chess album listed above.
■ **Heart Like Railroad Steel (Blues Ball)**
■ **Can't Put Me Out (Blues Ball)**
■ **From Early Till Late (Blue Night)**

Ditto, only more so. American bootlegs this time, with better sound, presumably because they're from stolen masters. All three albums contain a good deal of previously unreleased material, which is great news if, like me, you're a confirmed Wolf fanatic. The music is no great departure from what was already known, but it's a wonderful extension and in some cases a real revelation. My favorite of the three is **From Early Till Late**, essentially a bootleg of a bootleg, which contains five superlative sides from the Original Memphis Howlin' Wolf Orchestra together with a number of late 1950s cuts, then jumps to 1966 and 1968 from which a fragmentary but haunting solo "Rollin' and Tumblin' " emerges. **Heart Like Railroad Steel** and **Can't Put Me Out** divide up this same territory to some extent: the first covers the earlier ground, and the second starts in 1956, including the same version of "Rollin' and Tumblin'," and ending with a rousing live version of "Big House," recorded in 1972. Both of the Blues Ball albums duplicate the Syndicate Chapter to a very limited extent and the Blue Night issue a little more, but I wouldn't be without any of them.

■ **Change My Way (Chess Vintage)**

Nor would I be without this album (this is beginning to sound repetitive) consisting of singles from 1958 to 1966 that have for the most part been previously uncollected. Again, there may not be the consistency of the Greatest Hits compilation or of his first two albums for Chess, but once you're sold on Wolf, you're not going to want to miss anything, not even hearing him "Do the Do," an uptempo Willie Dixon-produced dance number, on which Wolf is at once ridiculous, intense (as always), and wonderful.

— HARP BLOWERS —

Sonny Boy Williamson
■ **This Is My Story (Chess: two-record set)**

The same story as with the other Chess two-record sets. This one consists of selections from **Down and Out Blues**, **The Real Folk Blues**, and **More Real Folk Blues**, and twenty-three of the twenty-four selections are written by Sonny Boy, with his unique combination of social *reportage* and mordant wit. As with Muddy and Wolf double sets, the individual albums are well worth getting (in this case **The Real Folk Blues** is perhaps the least compelling), but if you're looking for a selection that spans the breadth of Sonny Boy Williamson's remarkable career, this is it.

■ **Sonny Boy Williamson (Chess—Blues Masters Series: two-record set)**

I'm going to make a blanket endorsement here: Anything by Sonny Boy Williamson is worth getting. (This also holds for Howlin' Wolf, but not for Muddy Waters, say, an equally forceful performer and a far more influential one at his best.) This set was issued in 1976, and contains about an album's worth of material already familiar from **This Is My Story**. What is left contains several previously unissued selections and a number of hard-to-find items. There is no particular rhyme or reason to the anthology (it ranges from the beginning of Sonny Boy's career with Chess in 1955 until its end in 1963), but it shows Sonny Boy at his sly, witty, mythopoetic best. Highly recommended.

- **Bummer Road** (Chess—Vintage Series)
- **One Way Out** (Chess—Vintage Series)

Somewhat better-thought-out anthologies, from the days when Chess was Chess. Again, much previously unissued material (though a good deal of duplication with the Chess—Blues Masters set). **Bummer Road** contains a great studio dialogue in which Sonny Boy calls Leonard Chess a motherfucker, and Chess responds in kind. Catch the typically sharp Sonny Boy homiletics and Howlin' Wolf imitation on **One Way Out**. And don't forget the anthology of Sonny Boy's early Trumpet sides, **King Biscuit Time**, reissued on Arhoolie.

Walter Horton

- **Little Boy Blue** (JSP)

Walter Horton has never really made a great long-playing record under his own name (his greatest three minutes on record is "Easy," on **The Sun Box**). **Cotton Patch Hotfoots** (English Polydor), the collection of his early Memphis sides, is for aficionados only; his album with Johnny Young on Arhoolie, **Chicago Blues**, is lyrical but light; and his Alligator album with harmonica acolyte Carey Bell does not give much of an idea of the easy flow of invention that he shows both in an accompanying role and (sometimes) in live performance. **Little Boy Blue** is one of those special live performances in which Horton, playing in Boston with a pick-up band, for some reason catches fire and, equally improbably, there was someone there to record it. There are seven extended numbers—familiar tunes for the most part, and replete with Walter's typically chaotic vocals—but the only thing that matters is the harmonica, which is tough, lilting, demanding, occasionally breathtaking, and achingly bittersweet. There is no one like Walter Horton for mood, and if you have any interest in blues harmonica you should give this otherwise dispensable album a listen.

Little Walter

- **Boss Blues Harmonica** (Chess: two-record set)

The same holds here, except that this double album is indispensable, featuring back-up by the Muddy Waters band and the classic cuts upon which the foundation of modern blues harmonica playing rests. The first record consists entirely of what was previously titled **The Best of Little Walter** (Chess), and it is. "My Babe," "Last Night," "Blues With a Feeling," "Juke" are the standards against which every blues-harmonica player from Junior Wells to Paul Butterfield has measured himself, and they still hold up today as models of sound, feeling, virtuoso playing, and sheer technical invention. The second record is no less accomplished, only less familiar.

- **Confessin' the Blues** (Chess—Vintage Series)
- **Hate to See You Go** (Chess—Vintage Series)

More of the best of Little Walter. Once you're hooked, you're hooked, and there just isn't anything superfluous here. Great sides by Walter, with great support from Robert Jr. Lockwood and others.

Like the Wolf on Blues Ball and Blue Night, these are all bootlegs, presumably stolen from Chess in its late New Jersey days. I think they're less essential and less consistent than the albums listed previously, but not by much. If you already have the other albums, these three will provide a lot of alternate takes, which are certainly interesting if not necessary, but they also contain previously unissued material. On the latter two records, there are a good number of titles from 1962 on, which are really not worth much except to show Little Walter's sad decline.

Junior Wells
■ Blues Hit Big Town (Delmark)

Wells was a disciple of both Little Walter and Sonny Boy Williamson II, and these are his first sides, recorded in 1953 -1954 when he was nineteen and twenty years old. In some ways they remain the best of this almost-major bluesman, with classic titles like "Hoodoo Man" and rock-solid support from such friends and luminaries as Muddy Waters, Otis Spann, and Elmore James. Although Wells had not yet fully come into his own style, the songs that he performs here are among the very best he would ever write or record, and both his harp playing and vocals are without the troubling mannerisms that they would later develop. This is great blues from a figure whose prominence on the 1960s and 1970s white collector scene has somewhat obscured the reality of his contributions and somewhat misled Wells himself, too. "Blues Hit Big Town" and the acoustic demo "Please Throw This Poor Dog A Bone" are alone worth the price of admission.

Snooky Pryor
■ Snooky and Moody (Flyright)

Snooky Pryor was a mainstream harmonica player who emerged in the late 1940s under the strong influence of both Sonny Boy Williamsons. **Snooky and Moody** dates from Snooky's and Moody Jones's joint sessions for J.O.B. in the early 1950s and contains mostly unissued material. It is a masterpiece of mood with no musical masterpieces on it, touching, artless, almost ingenuous in its sheer musical transparency, the kind of record you can listen to over and over again without necessarily remembering titles but with images of Maxwell Street and Chicago in the late 1940s and early 1950s running through your mind.

—— PIANO PLAYERS ——

Otis Spann
- ■ Otis Spann is the Blues (Barnaby)
- ■ The Blues of Otis Spann (Black Cat; original issue on English Decca)
- ■ The Blues Never Die! (Prestige)
- ■ Heart Loaded With Trouble (Bluesway)

These are the best from what became a surprisingly prolific recording career in the last ten years of Spann's life. **Otis Spann is the Blues** was his first solo album, done in partnership with Robert Jr. Lockwood (it was Lockwood's first album, too). Lockwood's four vocals are unself-conscious recapitulations of the Robert Johnson style, and his contributions on guitar, which is the sole instrumental complement to Spann's piano, are, as usual, faultless. In many ways this is Spann's most personal album, with moving autobiographical compositions, fine solo piano on a couple of cuts, and an evident lack of calculation that is both touching and effective. **The Blues of**

Otis Spann was cut with the Muddy Waters band in England in 1964 and, despite the unfortunate use of what sounds like electric clarinet on a couple of cuts, is a true mirror of a great band and a great era for the blues. On **The Blues Never Die!** Spann shares vocals with Muddy Waters's long-time harmonica player James Cotton, and again the Muddy Waters band is featured. This time the band sound doesn't come across as strongly, perhaps because Cotton's harp isn't amplified, and Cotton's vocals, with the exception of "I Got a Feeling," are pretty much dispensable. Spann's contributions, on the other hand, are some of his best ever, and "The Blues Never Die" should forever stand as a deeply felt blues anthem. Finally, **Heart Loaded With Trouble** consists of the best of two 1966–1967 sessions featuring the then-current Muddy Waters band and, in essence, produced by Muddy himself. These are relaxed, easygoing sides for the most part, more extroverted than any of the other albums, with good new compositions by Spann and Muddy and St. Louis Jimmy and with classic titles like "My Home is in the Delta" and "Sarah Street."

Sunnyland Slim

■ **Sunnyland Slim (Flyright)**

From the golden period of Chicago blues, 1951–1955, featuring Slim as vocalist, Slim as instrumentalist, and Slim as accompanist—to the vocals of Johnny Shines and J.B. Lenoir. This is a consistently enjoyable and entertaining album, with large doses of Sunnyland Slim's plashing piano and some of the finest musicians of the blues' finest era.

─── COMMERCIAL TRENDS IN THE BLUES ───

Jimmy Reed

■ **Upside Your Head (Charly)**

■ **High and Lonesome (Charly)**

There have been innumerable reissues of Reed's enormously influential Vee Jay recordings. These are as good as any and are, at present, the most readily available. The first is a kind of "greatest hits" package, with "Bright Lights, Big City," "Ain't That Loving You, Baby?" "Big Boss Man," "Honest, I Do," "Baby, What You Want Me to Do?" and a host of others. If these titles don't mean anything to you, **High and Lonesome** would be just as good a choice, including his two earliest sides, a number of titles, both issued and unissued, from other early sessions, and as good a selection and as wide a variety as you're going to get from this somewhat limited artist. Reed is an ingratiating performer in small doses, and these albums provide a glimpse of his most attractive side before his music degenerated into self-parody.

13

B.B. King
and
T-Bone Walker

O ne thing has been left out in this account of the postwar blues boom and the improbable return to roots that accompanied it, and that is the birth of a brand-new blues style so pervasive today that it is virtually taken for granted and for many new listeners represents the only exposure to blues (through blues-influenced rock groups) that they are likely to get. This is the B.B. King school of the blues, whose single-string, treble-laden guitar work will characteristically explode in shimmering clusters of notes, embellishing, extending, but rarely supporting the vocal with the kind of full-bodied chords that derive from an older frailing style. This is the style favored by all the most popular contemporary blues stylists from Albert and Freddie King to Little Milton and Buddy Guy. It is the style adopted by innumerable anonymous studio musicians, black and white, when they want to play the blues. It is the subliminal flash of rock, the ripple beneath placid blues waters. And yet, like every other genre we have looked at in this book, it is a style that did not just spring up out of thin air but has a wealth of antecedents among the blues styles that we have seen.

B.B. King

B.B. King, the spearhead of this revolution, can himself boast of a classic background in the blues. Born Riley B. King in Mississippi in 1925, he came to Memphis in 1948 to make his living as a bluesman, at first moving in with his famous cousin, Bukka White. Through Sonny Boy Williamson (Rice Miller), he got his first radio job filling in for Sonny Boy on a West Memphis radio station, then broadcasting over WDIA, the Mother Station of the Negroes, where he was known as the Beale Street Blues Boy, later shortened simply to B.B. He recorded initially for Jim Bulleitt in Nashville, then for Sam Phillips, who leased his early sides to the Bihari Brothers and Modern Records in California. Robert Jr. Lockwood, one of the leading exponents of the progressive movement in Memphis, worked with him on his rhythm playing, something that B.B. never really perfected to the point of being able to play and sing at the same time. And he got his first full-scale public exposure at Memphis's Palace Theater, where

The young B.B. King molded an eclectic blues style from a wide variety of influences that included Ray Brown, Nat King Cole, and Frank Sinatra.
Courtesy of *Living Blues*

Rufus Thomas, the host of the Amateur Show, attests that he frequently appeared "with holes in his shoes, his guitar all patched up, just to get that dollar prize."

More than most blues singers, though, B.B. King was a self-made bluesman, with both the strengths and weaknesses that this implies. T-Bone Walker, it is true, exerted an incalculable influence, as he did upon almost every blues singer of the day, and it seems likely to me that T-Bone may well be the most underrated of all bluesmen, often cited but rarely listened to and still awaiting his rightful place in the blues pantheon. Nonetheless, even if Walker were given his full due, there is no question that B.B. King assembled his style from the most eclectic variety of sources. These sources included jazz and gospel, popular and country music as well as the blues, and perhaps this very eclecticism accounts as much as anything else for his unique susceptibility to white adaptation. In any case, his music is not—like that of Muddy Waters and Howlin' Wolf—the product of a local or isolated tradition, the inescapable extension of a long historical line. Instead, like the music of T-Bone Walker, it developed from a series of conscious choices that had to be made all the way down the line.

B.B. King's early music was very much influenced by the wide variety of material (everything from Count Basie to Frank Sinatra, Nat King Cole, Vaughn Monroe, and Frankie Laine) that he programmed as a disc jockey. To King, the theme of self-improvement has been a constant one, almost from childhood on, and he must have seen the radio not just as a chance to put himself across in a fifteen-minute live segment but as an opportunity to better himself both economically and musically as well. To that end, he soon acquired his own two-hour show; he taught himself to speak more properly; he widened his frame of musical reference; he updated his band from a typical Memphis boogie beat to the slick contemporary horn-dominated charts favored by the most up-to-the-minute jump bands of the day; and he also perfected the modest, almost self-deprecating, but self-assured manner that serves him to this day.

King put together his vocal style, it is clear, from his admiration for Roy Brown, whose gospel-influenced "crying" style revolutionized the jump blues of the late 1940s and provided the principal inspiration for Little Richard and James Brown in the 1950s. Gradually King found his own voice in a falsetto-edged modification of Brown's soaring tenor with the full-throated phlegminess, dramatic emotionalism, and heavy use of melisma (stretching a single syllable over several notes) of the fervid quartet singer. He drew heavily too on the declamatory manner of Louis Jordan, whose popeyed vocals were used more for comedy, while B.B.'s were the stuff of heavy drama. And his guitar—while in his early work, he was still fumbling a little for a style, he soon adopted a sound and a tone all his own as he combined elements from the work of Lonnie Johnson, Lowell Fulson, and, of course, T-Bone Walker with the jazz playing of Charlie Christian and Django Reinhardt.

Even B.B.'s repertoire was drawn from an eclectic variety of sources. His first records were made in 1949, but his first big hit came in 1951–1952 with "Three O'Clock Blues," which, unlike any of the downhome hits, went to the number one spot and remained on the charts for seventeen weeks. Like nearly all of his later hits, "Three O'Clock" was not original with B.B., but had been a very popular song for its composer, Lowell Fulson, some two years earlier. "Every Day I Have the Blues" came from Fulson as well, "How Blue Can You Get?" from Louis Jordan, "Rock Me Mama" from Arthur Crudup and Lil Son Jackson, even "Sweet Little Angel," the song with which he became most identified, from Tampa Red via Robert Nighthawk. It's all somewhat academic, for at this point these are all B.B. King's songs, transmuted by an instantly recognizable style that has been polished to a high gloss and by a popularity that has far surpassed anything any previous blues singer achieved. Muddy Waters and John Lee Hooker were, in a sense, flukes of the marketplace, but B.B. King was a *star* who eventually played Las Vegas, performed on the Ed Sullivan Show, and enjoyed what may have been the blues' first Top Forty pop hit with Roy Hawkins's "The Thrill Is Gone." Always his assimilating intelligence managed to transform into his own style what could have been merely slavish copies. All through his career B.B. King's goals have been to move ahead with the times while keeping his feet firmly planted in the past. Even today, long after international success has placed him in a category all his own, King continues to listen to and cite country bluesmen like his cousin Bukka White and Blind Lemon Jefferson, and it remains one of his abiding goals to record an album of classic blues titles by such artists as Jefferson, Leroy Carr, and Lonnie Johnson. And his guitar playing, so familiar by now that it seems almost cliched, remains the fount from which all the Mike Bloomfields, Eric Claptons, Johnny Winters have sprung. And yet, it was as much as of a breakthrough in its conception of the guitar as a solo instrument as Little Walter's harmonica work was when it first burst upon the blues scene.

Nonetheless, B.B. King would undoubtedly be the first to credit T-Bone Walker as his primary influence and the chief inspiration for his own single-string, controlled-dynamics guitar style. No matter how many separate sources might be listed in a delineation of the origins of King's style, no matter how eclectic a range of influences and genres King might have sought out, it was the mellow-toned, lightly swinging, guitar-led blues of T-Bone Walker that first established the modern blues sound and exerted a dominant influence, not only on B.B. King but on nearly every other postwar bluesman, from Lightnin' Hopkins to Muddy Waters to the hot guitarists of Memphis and Chicago.

T-Bone Walker

Aaron Thibeaux Walker was a second-generation bluesman who was born in Linden, Texas in 1910 and died in Los Angeles in 1975. His life spanned the documented history of the blues, and he himself first recorded as a teenager in a style that was reminiscent of Blind Lemon Jefferson, one of his earliest mentors, whom he led around Dallas in the 1920s. Along with Charlie Christian, with whom he played as a young man and with whom he must share credit for introducing the widespread use of the electric guitar, he came out of the Territory bands (Texas-Oklahoma-Kansas) and was featured vocalist with Les Hite and His Orchestra in the late 1930s and early 1940s. In 1947, he recorded his own composition, "Call It Stormy Monday (But Tuesday Is Just as Bad)", which became one of the all-time blues standards and a staple in just about every major bluesman's act. He was renowned as a showman who electrified the Apollo Theater with practiced splits, behind-the-back guitar tricks, and a polished stage act that proved to be a great influence on the young Elvis Presley, not to mention an equally impressionable Chuck Berry. He was also responsible for a revolution in blues guitar playing.

Listen to his records today. While the lyrics of his songs are often simply clever or high-flown ("I was born with emotions, and a song was in my soul," declares one, not atypically), the guitar sound is as accessible as it was Walker's heyday, possessing the same clarity of conception, the same fluidity of touch that must first have struck contemporary listeners. It is a remarkable feat of retrospection to listen to T-Bone Walker after the fact and hear so many of the ideas of B.B. King, Chuck Berry, Robert Jr. Lockwood, Freddie King fully realized years before any of them achieved their mature style. The long fluid lines, the cascades of single notes at the treble end of the scale, the rhythmic assurance and delicate, almost feathery touch—above all, the drama of his playing, with its characteristically dark overtures and ascending and descending clusters of seventh and ninth chords—have lost none of their freshness of conception or sound, are as convincing right now as they were in 1947. "T-Bone Walker has a touch that nobody has been able to duplicate," said B.B. King. "I can still hear T-Bone in my mind today, from that first record I heard, 'Stormy Monday'. He was the first electric guitar player I heard on record. . . . [It was] the prettiest sound I think I ever heard in all my life. . . . He made me so that I knew I just *had* to go out and get an electric guitar."

A whole generation took up electric guitar after listening to T-Bone. Walker introduced Gatemouth Brown to Don Robey of Duke Records, for whom Brown recorded some of the finest T-Bone-influenced sides of the 1950s. Bobby "Blue" Bland modeled his band and his whole musical concept on the mellow sound of T-Bone Walker ("He wasn't a great singer, really, but he was a great stylist,"

T-Bone Walker, author of "Stormy Monday," perfected the single-string, hornlike sound of electric blues guitar.
Courtesy of *Living Blues*

says Bland). Lowell Fulson's sophisticated swing sprang directly from hearing T-Bone Walker's records. All over Texas, Oklahoma, California, in Memphis and Chicago, too, guitarists sprang up imitating that sound. And B.B. King, who learned at T-Bone's feet, exported that sound to the world, transforming himself in the process from race recording star to international blues idol.

SELECTED RECORDINGS

B.B. King
- **Rock Me Baby (United)**
- **16 Original Big Hits (Fantasy)**

His greatest hits from the twelve-year period with RPM/Modern/Kent/United. For the Memphis era and the B.B. King style in embryo, check out **B.B. King, 1949–1950** (listed in the Memphis section of Chapter X). For the later period it's a toss-up between these two. Both offer "Three O'Clock Blues," "Sweet Sixteen," "Sweet Little Angel," and "Everyday I Have the Blues," along with four more shared titles. The Fantasy release omits "Rock Me Baby"; United leaves out "My Own Fault, Baby." I think I would probably choose the Fantasy, because there are a couple more titles and because there are a number of selections which I've always found exceptionally tasteful and delicate in their guitar work and gracious in their acknowledgment of the influence of Sleepy John Estes, Cecil Gant, and Lonnie Johnson. You can't go wrong with either album, though; one or the other is the place to start, the cornerstone of any B.B. King collection.

- **Live at the Regal (ABC/MCA)**

Recorded in Chicago in 1964 with a tight little band (the Modern sides are more big and swing band-oriented) and a very enthusiastic audience. Many of the titles here are the same as on the two albums listed above, but this is a whole different ballgame. Though

B.B.'s voice is a little ragged and by 1964 he could no longer hit the falsetto notes, **Live at the Regal** remains one of the classic live albums, ranking up there with **James Brown Live at the Apollo** and **Jerry Lee Lewis Live Just About Anywhere** in giving a sense of the true ambience of the music. I would be hard put to choose between this and the United or Fantasy album. I wouldn't want to give up either one, but there is no question in my mind that this is the one I would pick if all the blues clubs folded and I wanted to remind myself of what it was *really* like to listen to the blues.

■ Blues Is King (ABC/MCA)

Another live album, this time recorded in a more intimate setting, at the International Club in Chicago, in 1966 with a small organ-led group and an exceptional degree of recording clarity. Though King's vocals are more stentorian here, verging on the kind of full-throated bellowing that he favors today, the guitar work is brilliant—fluid, imaginative, witty without falling into the trap of overembroidery. Song selection is good, and energy is at a peak. Aficionados who know better than I (Dick Shurman) feel that this represents a pinnacle of King's recorded guitar style, and it probably does.

T-Bone Walker

■ T-Bone Jumps Again (Charly)
■ T-Bone Walker (Blue Note: two-record set)

The best collections of his early singles. The first spans the years 1942–1949 and includes both his earliest hit ("Mean Old World") and his best-known number ("Stormy Monday"). This is easy listening of the best sort—blues, shuffles, and jumps—highly polished, highly stylized performances that have dated somewhat in their hip lingo but scarcely at all in their musical approach. The Blue Note album was cut for Imperial between 1950 and 1954 and is an equally attractive combination: good songs, good feeling, and a remarkable foreshadowing of all sorts of by-now-familiar trends in the blues.

■ T-Bone Blues (Atlantic)

Recorded later, though not by much. This was cut with all-star line-ups in Chicago and Los Angeles in 1955, 1956, and 1959. Unfortunately, it represented T-Bone's last recordings of any significance and, except for a single session in 1964, he didn't even enter a recording studio again until 1966. Here he has a chance to stretch out with some fine studio and jazz musicians, trading solos with Barney Kessel and pianist Lloyd Glenn on a collection of some of his best and best-known tunes. In many ways this may be the easiest introduction to T-Bone's work, offering a thoughtful context in which to place his always impeccable musicianship and tasteful delivery.

14

Post-Modernism: Chicago

The B.B. King/T-Bone Walker school took hold all over the country. In California, it became the dominant mode at an early date, although, as with jazz, it was in a cooler vein with neither the heat nor the gospel-laced passion that B.B. King imparted to it. In Chicago, too, the style took hold, and it was here that blues made what will very likely be its last stand as a popular music.

In the early 1950s the Muddy Waters band was the undisputed standard against which every major bluesman measured himself. Even Howlin' Wolf, for all his fierce individuality and deep-seated Memphis roots, sought a rough approximation of the formula established by Waters and Chess Records, though his own sound remained unique. By the late 1950s, though, Muddy Waters had become old-fashioned and Wolf practically prehistoric, and it was the much more up-to-date (and much more popular) B.B. King style that had become the model for any self-respecting, up-and-coming musician. By the early 1960s, the blues world was full of King sound alikes, and there was a whole string of prominent Kings (Albert, Freddie, B.B. Jr.), many of whom invoked familial as well as stylistic relationships. It was a trio of Chicago bluesmen who emerged in the mid-1950s, however, who took the new style about as far as it would go and then settled back (in two cases) into an uncomfortable middle age of their own.

Buddy Guy, Otis Rush, and Magic Sam all were born between 1934 and 1937 and arrived in Chicago while still in their teens—Guy from Louisiana, Rush and Sam (Maghett) from Mississippi. All three recorded for Eli Toscano's Cobra and Artistic labels to begin with, when they were barely twenty years old, and while none had the widespread hits of Freddie or Albert King or even Little Milton, each contributed a new element to the make-up of the blues, and each extended the territory a little bit more.

Otis Rush

Otis Rush was the oldest by a couple of years and the first to record by a couple of months. He came into the Cobra studio in 1956 under the sponsorship of Willie Dixon who, by virtue of his success as a composer (he had written most of Muddy Waters's and Howlin' Wolf's biggest hits) and session master, had become the leading black blues entrepreneur in Chicago. He contributed a number of songs to Rush's sessions over the next couple of years, but the remarkable thing about Rush's output for Cobra (sixteen titles in all) was how fully formed Rush's own style was, how deeply felt and expressed were his own original compositions, and how complete and mature a body of work he managed to put together in a little more than two years of recording. Songs like "Groaning the Blues," "Double Trouble" ("Some of this generation is millionaires/it's hard for me to even keep decent clothes to wear") "Three Times a Fool," and "I Can't Quit You, Baby" combined music and lyrics, the customized sound of B.B. King without the emphasis on pyrotechnics many of Rush's generation adopted, and a vocal virtuosity rarely heard in contemporary blues. Almost like Robert Johnson, Rush would sing in his natural range, at the *top* of his natural range, and then employ a break in his voice to slide into an effortless falsetto. It was the pure emotionalism of Mississippi combined with an exquisite approach to phrasing, a clear, rounded guitar tone that rivaled T-Bone Walker's, and an aspiration to jazz (Wes Montgomery and Kenny Burrell remain Rush's idols), all harnessed to a sense of the blues that Muddy Waters has used to illustrate his concept of "deep blues." Rush was among the first, too, to emphasize blues in a minor key, a genre that became almost commonplace with the later recordings of Bobby "Blue" Bland but that had previously been relegated to vaudeville and orchestrated blues numbers. All in all, the small body of work that he recorded for Cobra is virtually unmatched in modern times and could be compared with some justice to the two isolated sessions of Robert Johnson except for the fact that Rush himself survived.

Rush's career over the last twenty years (his final Cobra session was in 1958) is a painful tale of failure—professional, creative, and personal. None of his record contracts has worked out, he has never added substantially to the body of his work, and it's impossible to say at this point what exactly led to his breakthrough or, conversely, what has dammed him up. Nonetheless, Otis Rush's earliest sides will continue to stand as a monument to the last best hope of the modernist movement.

Magic Sam

Magic Sam was something of a protege of Rush's and came to Cobra through his friend. Unlike Rush, he did not possess the spark of genius, but his whipcord, vibrato-laden voice conveyed emotion and excitement, and his stinging B.B. King-styled guitar cut through the simple, pared-down arrangements with some of the forcefulness of a young Muddy Waters. Of the ten titles he recorded for Cobra, three were to the tune of "All Your Love," a brooding, intense, and very much Otis Rush-influenced minor-key blues. After he got out of the Army in 1961, he recorded for a number of different small labels in a smattering of different styles until, in 1968, he recorded for Delmark, the first major bluesman to record for a collector label after

Junior Wells. The records that he made for Delmark, unlike Otis Rush's later efforts, are a reflection of a mature style, a combination of the boogie beat of John Hooker, the minor-key blues and "West Side soul" that Otis Rush had pioneered, the ensemble sound of Muddy Waters, and the driving energy of Magic Sam. Like many of the other Chicago bluesmen, he played at the 1969 Ann Arbor Blues Festival and made a tremendous hit with the young white audience, picking up college bookings all over the country and seemingly ready to launch a whole new career when he died at the age of thirty-two a few months after the festival.

Buddy Guy

Buddy Guy, the third of the triumvirate, is by far the best-known, both by virtue of his long association with Junior Wells (which gained him a large measure of white acclaim in the blues revival of the 1960s) and due to his earlier connection with Chess Records all through the first half of the 1960s. Guy, in fact, left Artistic, Cobra's sister label, after only two releases to become Chess's last blues star, making excitingly emotional records of his own and providing older artists like Howlin' Wolf and Muddy Waters with contemporary back-up from his well-disciplined band. Considerably more intense than either Otis Rush or Magic Sam, Guy also modeled himself most closely on B.B. King, to the point that he was fearful that B.B. would sue him when his first record came out. His early records combine frenetic falsetto vocals with screaming lead guitar, and there is little that is more immediately dramatic in contemporary blues than Guy's reworkings of such traditional material as Little Brother Montgomery's "First Time I Met the Blues" or Willie Dixon's "When My Left Eye Jumps." Unfortunately, and perhaps not surprisingly, Guy was not able to sustain this level of emotionalism for long, and following his departure from Chess in 1966, his career, somewhat like Rush's, became an object lesson in the pitfalls of early success. Never again has he attained the heights or the unabashed intensity of his early sides; not only voice, but energy and focus, too, seem to have burned out.

In subsequent years, others have built on the base that Otis Rush, Magic Sam, and Buddy Guy laid down. Thoughtful artists like Fenton Robinson and Jimmy Dawkins, Son Seals and Jimmy Johnson have carried on the tradition, fusing the sound of B.B. King, T-Bone Walker, pop jazz, and the upbeat rhythms of contemporary soul to form the characteristic sound of West Side soul. For the most part, though, their records have never really been popular, mainly reaching a collector's market in which 10,000-album sales is a high-water mark and never influencing, and thereby extending, the mainstream blues tradition in the way that Rush, Sam, and Buddy Guy once did.

SELECTED RECORDINGS

Albert King
- Born Under a Bad Sign (Stax)
- Years Gone By (Stax)

The best of the last truly popular mainstream bluesmen, whose style was formed by B.B. King and who in turn has vastly influenced such contemporary stylists as Otis Rush, Son Seals, Jimmy Johnson, and Magic Slim. His guitar is somewhat different than B.B.'s, shriller and sometimes punchier as well, more metallic in tone but with a grittier taste; his vocals are soulful, with a curiously delicate quality of their own; and his material on these two albums (including such hits as "Crosscut Saw," and "Laundromat Blues" as well as blues ballads like "The Very Thought Of You" and "As the Years Go Passing By") is uniformly excellent. Nice listening, good mood music, though, like anything in the strictly single-string, B.B. King guitar style, it can grow wearing after a while.

Freddie King

■ Freddie King (King/Gusto)

This King had a bunch of hits in the early 1960s, mostly instrumentals with snappy rhythms and catchy melodies, but he was a fine singer as well. This seventeen-cut album contains his earliest and best vocals ("Lonesome Whistle," "I'm Tore Down"), along with better-known instrumental hits like "Hide Away" and "San-Ho-Zay." In later years he became one of the most successful fusion (black singer, white band) artists, and the music responded by taking on an overwrought quality of its own; but here he is relaxed, good-natured, having a good time, and turning out blues that were highly influential both to his contemporaries and to a later generation.

Otis Rush

■ Groaning the Blues (Flyright)

These are the classic Cobra sides. There's not much to say about them, except that they represent a pinnacle in modern blues. The album is marred, unfortunately, by the inclusion of every title that Rush cut (*every* title was not a classic). In some cases, a previously unissued take is substituted for the more familiar version, and a number of the alternate takes do not differ sufficiently to warrant the duplication. To confuse matters even further, a second album entitled **Otis Rush and Magic Sam: The Other Takes (Flyright)** includes more unissued materials, along with the missing Cobra takes. Sound is not particularly good on either album, but stick to **Groaning the Blues** for the best of Otis Rush and the best of contemporary blues singing.

Magic Sam

■ Magic Rocker (Flyright)

Some of the same comments appy to this as to the Otis Rush Cobra album listed above. All ten of Sam's Cobra titles (plus a couple of alternate takes) are here, along with two by his "cousin," Shakey Jake, on which Sam plays guitar. There is a side of great music here, including Shakey Jake's two numbers, which feature some of Sam's most exciting guitar work, but discographical completeness works against artistic effect. This is an album that you really should have for its highpoints, but you should also be prepared to overlook about half of it.

■ West Side Soul (Delmark)

A great album, a high point of blues recording for the collector market. Everything about this album works, from the ragged piano playing of Stockholm Slim (Swedish pianist Per Notini, who just happened to be in town) to the fire and focus with which Sam approaches every song. Some sessions just seem to be inspired, and this was one of them, creating a whole new genre of music not so much for the players (this is *club* music, after all) but for its *nouveau arrivé* listeners. Just to show what a difference inspiration can make, Sam made a later album for Delmark called **Black Magic** in which almost all the same elements are present. It is respectable enough, it is unquestionably Magic Sam, but equally unquestionably the thrill is gone on this particular date.

■ **Magic Sam Live (Delmark: two-record set)**

A powerful set consisting of recordings made at the 1969 Ann Arbor Festival and the Alex Club on Chicago's West Side. The Ann Arbor set, long anticipated and finally due to be released in early 1982, bears out Sam's reputation as a crowd pleaser and surpasses even the explosive energy level of the studio Delmark release. The second record explores less familiar territory, as rock 'n' roll, soul, and jazz are all touched on and the downhome atmosphere of a club brings out another side of Magic Sam without ever taking away from the excitement or impact of the music. Both dates are recorded in very low fi, but that shouldn't matter for a moment.

Buddy Guy

■ **I Was Walking Through the Woods (Chess)**

This is *the* contemporary Chicago blues album, if you except the Otis Rush Flyright album for the reasons mentioned above and consider **West Side Soul** in a slightly different category. I get cold chills every time I listen. Hysteria, pandemonium, wild beauty, and transcendence are present in abundance. Plus Buddy Guy's shattering voice and guitar. Some might call it overwrought, but to me it's the drama of high art.

■ **A Man and the Blues (Vanguard)**

Latter-day Buddy Guy—only a few years later but in a new, more restrained manner. Of all the post-Chess albums by Guy (and there are a good number) this is by far the best—tasteful, somewhat introspective, and with a truly great band led by Otis Spann—but somehow it's still not the same as the unrestricted, unabashed, and probably sometimes unrehearsed fervor of the Chess sides.

Jimmy Dawkins

■ **All for Business (Delmark)**

One of the few records strictly in the Otis Rush school. Dawkins is no vocalist (Big Voice Odom, otherwise known as B.B. Jr., handles most of the vocals here), but these are wonderful original compositions by Dawkins with a great band (sparked by Otis Rush on second guitar) and much of the somber mood of Rush's best sides. Like a number of albums mentioned in the chapter on Chicago blues, this is a case of a second-line bluesman putting out music of the first order. Dawkins is not an artist to stay with too long, since he tends to repeat themes and motifs (and songs), but this was an inspired session.

Fenton Robinson

■ **Somebody Loan Me a Dime (Alligator)**

■ **I Hear Some Blues Downstairs (Alligator)**

The originator of one of the most thoughtful offshoots of the T-Bone

Walker style on the South Side, Robinson has yet to make a record that fully lives up to his potential. There are good songs on both these records (including such well-known originals as "Somebody Loan Me a Dime" and the Peppermint Harris-authored "As the Years Go Passing By"), the performances are tasteful without exception, and the musicianship is of a uniformly high caliber—but the spark is simply not there. At least not yet.

Son Seals
■ Midnight Son (Alligator)

Son Seals is the one post-B.B. King black bluesman to achieve widespread popularity with a white audience. This was his second album for the collector label, Alligator, and will probably stand as his best blues contribution, since on subsequent offerings he has gone in a harder, more rock-oriented direction. Here he maintains his Magic Sam/Albert King roots (he played with King as a drummer and second guitarist for several years) and contributes a number of strong original songs on his own. There's lots of energy here, there's a strong blues heritage, and a willingness to go off in new and exploratory directions. On his first album his vocals sounded very much like Magic Sam's; here he sounds more like Muddy, with a throaty growl that on later albums has become something of a mannerism, and a hard-edged, metallic guitar sound that can grow grating after a while.

Jimmy Johnson
■ Johnson's Whacks (Delmark)
■ Living Chicago Blues Vol. 1 (Alligator)

Punning, funny, inventive, exploratory of many different genres (rockabilly, country, soul music, blues), this is an album for all seasons, its only drawback being its very diversity. Johnson was fifty years old when he made this debut record, and it seems as if he was just bursting with energy and ideas. You can hear traces of Otis Rush and Magic Sam (with whom Johnson's brother, Mac Thompson, played bass for many years), you can even catch strains of Tyrone Davis, Little Milton, and Bobby "Blue" Bland, but when you get down to the real nitty-gritty, it's all Jimmy Johnson. This 1978 album is one of the bravest blues experiments in recent years by a talent who has long been on the scene but who would never have seem capable of such radical experimentation. If you want to catch a glimpse of his more conventional side, get hold of **Living Chicago Blues**, Vol. 1 on which Johnson does a set of standards in customarily vigorous and exultatory fashion.

— 15 —

Going Down South (Again)

All through the South and out in California as well as in Chicago, small labels continued to spring up in the 1940s, 1950s, and 1960s, either dedicated to the downhome sound or with scattered downhome titles showing up among their more sophisticated jazz, rhythm and blues, and rock'n'roll offerings. This was merely another variation of the postwar blues boom, whereby a folk culture's limited life was extended in time and geography both by an easier access to technology and by the dispersion of an audience that was nostalgic for the downhome sounds. The result was rhythm and blues hits of the unlikeliest sort, from Wilbert Harrison's 1959 smash "Kansas City" to Little Johnny Taylor's 1963 "Part Time Love" on the West Coast Galaxy label.

Memphis, of course, was a hotbed of small labels. In Detroit, the success of John Lee Hooker led to a profusion of small companies, and almost all of them recorded Hooker at one time or another. In Mississippi and Arkansas, too, talent was being scouted as it had not been since the 1920s, and if the bluesmen were not brought in to Memphis to record, they might well be recorded in the field. In fact, the blues was getting a hearing all over the map, but nowhere was it confirmed as a greater commercial success or a more fruitful hybrid than in New Orleans.

New Orleans has always been a kind of special case with the blues. If you were to ask the casual observer, New Orleans would probably be named the birthplace of the blues as often as not, but except for instrumental blues (jazz), there was never really a strong downhome tradition before World War II, even though all New Orleans music is suffused with a lazy melodic sense of the blues. In fact, even in the postwar years New Orleans continued to present the most eclectic mix of musical styles and approaches. Whole books could be written about the intertwining of various traditions in New Orleans—and indeed several have—but from a pure blues point of view a number of traditions in particular stand out.

One is the piano blues style made popular by Fats Domino in the 1950s but with its roots in boogie woogie, jump blues, and older New Orleans traditions. There were a whole raft of legendary New Orleans

Professor Longhair was a musical eccentric whose playful sense of craziness was all his own.
Courtesy of *Living Blues*

pianists from Domino himself to Salvador Doucette, Huey "Piano" Smith, Lloyd Price, Archibald, Clarence "Frogman" Henry, and later Allen Toussaint and James Booker, all of whom could, and often did, stand in for each other. Each of these artists made his own significant contribution to New Orleans music, but it was Professor Longhair, both the inspiration for, and the one true maverick from, this whole school who was the real original.

Professor Longhair

Longhair, born Henry Roeland Byrd in Bogalusa, Louisiana, in 1918, was as eccentric as his stage name would suggest (he was first dubbed Professor Longhair, and his band the Shuffling Hungarians, when he shaved his head in the late 1940s). A tapdancer to begin with, he combined the rhythms of his dance with rock, roll, rhumba, boogie, calypso, and totally spontaneous improvisations of his own to create a music that was decidedly New Orleans but altogether Longhair—a blues that was playful, joyous, crazy in the best sense of the word, and that achieved a kind of sophisticated primitivism (or was that primitive sophistication?) that you will find in no other bluesman and that will make you smile again and again. "Now the thing about Professor Longhair," said New Orleans saxophonist Alvin "Red" Tyler, "is that his piano playing is unorthodox. You know, usually with a trained musician we have a certain pattern we are going to follow. . . . He would throw them all out the window. . . . The things he did were so unorthodox until when he'd do some of these things it would just amuse you. You understood what he was doing, but it was really unorthodox, and it was a gas."

Smiley Lewis

New Orleans had its own resident blues shouters, too. Big Joe Turner lived in town for many years, and Roy Brown was born there. But it was Smiley Lewis who possessed that "pleasing" touch that best characterized the New Orleans sound, driving, rhythmic, but melodically and personally ingratiating at the same time. Like Fats Domino, Lewis, who was born Overton Amos Lemons in 1920, recorded for Imperial and, after Domino, may well have been their most popular New Orleans artist. His biggest hits were "I Hear You Knocking" and "One Night," which, like his classic "Blue Monday," became more widely identified later with other artists (Fats Domino, Elvis Presley), but he also originated songs like "Big Mamou" and "Shame Shame Shame," the theme from the motion picture *Baby Doll*. Like his stylistic mentors Big Joe Turner and Wynonie Harris, Lewis possessed a full-bodied shouter's voice, but he also had the warmth and rhythmic flexibility that were particularly characteristic of New Orleans. He incorporated blues, cajun, big-voiced ballads, and rock'n'roll into a typically infectious amalgam that remained pretty much the same—sometimes with backing from Fats Domino's band, sometimes with less celebrated but equally adept New Orleans musicians—right up until the time of his death in 1966.

Guitar Slim

None of these styles, however charming, could be classified as hard blues, though. If you were looking for *hard* blues in New Orleans in the 1950s, Guitar Slim was your man. Guitar Slim, born Eddie Jones in Greenwood, Mississippi, in 1926, deserves mention in any history of popular music if for only one reason: his connection with Ray Charles and the development of Charles's enormously influential gospel-based style. By 1954, Jones had already recorded for Imperial and for Bullet in Nashville when he was signed to the newly resurgent Specialty label, which was just about to see success with the New Orleans-based rock'n'roll of Lloyd Price and Little Richard. In New Orleans, Jones hooked up with Ray Charles, who had already cut quite a bit on his own out on the West Coast but had been gigging around New Orleans as a piano player for some time. On September 26, Slim had a session for Specialty during which he cut six or seven titles. One of them was "The Things That I Used to Do," a blues that probably sold hundreds of thousands in its day but remains one of the most influential and popular deep blues standards. The pianist and arranger for the session was Ray Charles.

Guitar Slim was in many ways the antithesis of all that Ray Charles had sought to become in his musical career up to that time. Crude, untutored, musically unsophisticated, possessed of a primitive, perfervid style that most resembled the gospel shouting of the Baptist church and changed little from song to song, Slim must have come as something of a revelation to Ray Charles—still in the Charles Brown/Nat King Cole bag—of something that he had known all along. Indeed the arrangement and the mode of Guitar Slim's hit, with its church-borrowed changes, horns riffing like a soulful choir, and emotionally charged vocals, would set the pattern for much of Ray Charles's subsequent career and the startling impact he was to have on the world of popular music. For Guitar Slim, on the other hand, there were only a few more sessions before his popularity ran out and he was dropped by Specialty, to die at the age of thirty-three in 1959.

Clifton Chenier

Another more durable, and more idiosyncratic, Louisiana-based

Clifton Chenier virtually invented zydeco, a music derived from rural roots and popular stylings, deeply ingrained Acadian traditions, and contemporary rhythm and blues.
Courtesy of *Living Blues*

stylist, who was recorded by Specialty early on and has since enjoyed a long, zestful, and highly acclaimed career of his own, was Clifton ·Chenier. Chenier, known as the King of Zydeco, virtually invented a brand-new blues music from rural roots and popular stylings, deeply-ingrained Acadian traditions, and contemporary rhythm and blues. Zydeco, in the first place, is a black adaptation of cajun music (the music of the transplanted Acadians), with accordion as the lead instrument and a form of fractured French (cajun) as the principal language. The origin of the style is somewhat shrouded in mystery, and even the origin of the term "zydeco" is somewhat problematic (it is supposed to have come from a phonetic shortening of the title of an old zydeco tune, "Les Haricots sont pas sale"), but the spirit of the music is clear: good times and good fun, bop till you drop, and don't, under any circumstances, *ever* look back. The music was made up mostly of waltzes and two-steps and fiddle-accordion country tunes until Clifton Chenier, born in Opelousas in 1925, came along and started recording, first for Californian J.R. Fullbright's Elko and Post labels, then for Specialty, which was riding the crest of the rock'n'roll wave at the time. Chenier, always the most dazzling of eclecticists, played driving rock'n'roll like "Boppin' the Rock" on the accordion, and many of his earliest recordings sound derivative, if not imitative, of popular tunes of the day. As his own style deepened, particularly in the 1960s when he started recording for the folk label Arhoolie, he claimed more and more of this territory as his own, with a repertoire that showed off hard blues, rocking instrumentals, rhythm and blues flavored tunes, even country-and-western numbers translated into French, all synthesized and comprehended within the same unique, hard-driving style. A couple of live albums indicate the energy of a high-spirited, good-rocking, all-night dance, which is, after all, what the music was designed for in the first place, and singers like Boozoo Chavis, Rockin Dopsie, and Fernest Arceneaux have all followed in Chenier's pioneering footsteps. For the last few years, wherever Chenier has performed, he has worn a gaudy, jewel-encrusted crown, which symbolizes his reign as the undisputed king of zydeco.

The Excello Sound

More conventional in terms of blues was the output of a Nashville-based company called Excello, which from 1955 to 1965 got most of its blues output from a record store owner in Crowley, Louisiana, named Jay Miller. It was Miller who unearthed artists like Lightnin' Slim, Slim Harpo, Lonesome Sundown, Silas Hogan, and Lazy Lester, and in the process documented a regional style with as much cohesiveness and commitment to roots as anything outside of Memphis or Chicago. The Excello sound was in its own way quite influential, representing a holdover of downhome blues (the fact that downhome blues was able to survive at all in the wake of rock'n'roll was significant) and presenting a form of music, "swamp blues," that differed from previous blues trends and heavily influenced white artists like Tony Joe White, Donnie Fritts, and even Charlie Rich. In addition to giving colorful names to his artists, Miller made a real musical contribution as well, writing songs, carefully rehearsing the studio band, altering tempos, frequently using woodblocks for a distinctive percussion sound, and generally producing records much in the way that Leonard Chess and Sam Phillips were doing with more mainstream music.

Miller's two most important artists—certainly his most commercially successful—were Lightnin' Slim (Otis Hicks) and Slim Harpo (James Moore). Lightnin' Slim, who took his name from the obvious source, got his music from a combination of the Lightnin' Hopkins and Muddy Waters sounds that were so popular in the mid-1950s. With his heavy, almost sagging voice and very rudimentary guitar accompaniment set off by the harmonica of Slim Harpo or Lazy Lester, Lightnin' Slim created a slurred style that even on remakes of popular songs like Muddy Waters's "Mannish Boy" or Lightnin' Hopkins's "My Starter Won't Work," remained distinctly, if repetitiously, his own. Slim Harpo was at one and the same time more conventional and more original than Lightnin' Slim. Playing guitar and rack harmonica simultaneously, much in the manner of Jimmy Reed, Slim Harpo patterned his whole sound on the pervasive style of Reed, as did much of the Excello stable. This was modified, however, by the characteristically dark sound of Excello, which has most often been characterized as "doomy" and even on the relatively light-hearted efforts of Slim Harpo maintains a heavier beat and a more somber coloration than the lighter tones of Reed himself. Miller also had the inspiration to get Slim Harpo to sing through his nose in a pinched, nasal tone that gives most of his records an immediately distinctive and instantly recognizable sound. In person, he often sang in a more conventional, perfectly acceptable blues-flavored voice, but his biggest hits on record—"I'm a King Bee," "Scratch My Back," "Tip On In"—leap out at the listener by their strange combination of mode and message, almost as if a black country-and-western singer or a white rhythm and blues singer were attempting to impersonate a member of the opposite genre. Perhaps not surprisingly, one of the most successful cover versions of a Slim Harpo song was an early recording of "I'm a King Bee" by the Rolling Stones, whose vocalist, Mick Jagger, used Slim Harpo's whining tone as a take-off for a new amalgam of his own.

Robert Pete Williams

On an altogether different plane, Robert Pete Williams, a native of the Baton Rouge area who had played at house parties and local gatherings for years with Slim Harpo, Lonesome Sundown, and Silas Hogan, created a blues style that was absolutely unique and that is hard to imagine getting a hearing in any jook joint or barrelhouse where the blues was ordinarily heard. Williams was found in 1958 by folklorist Harry Oster doing life for murder on the same Angola Prison Farm where Leadbelly had been discovered twenty-five years before. Oster recorded Williams in the prison yard singing blues improvised for the most part around the theme of his imprisonment. There were birds chirping in the background, and on one song, "Prisoner's Talking Blues," Williams reminisced, "Some of the prisoners there, they couldn't stand it, and so I had to cut it off. All them prisoners, standing around crying, thinking about their homes. They made me stop singing."

Williams gained his release from prison through his music and made his first public appearance outside of Louisiana at the same 1964 Newport Folk Festival which saw the debuts of Fred McDowell, Skip James, Sleepy John Estes, and Mississippi John Hurt before a large-scale white audience. Unlike McDowell and Hurt, and the others to a lesser extent, Williams never gained much of a following among this new audience, both because his music was so intensely personal and because he was not playing in any certifiable tradition. Almost alone among recorded blues singers, Robert Pete Williams seems to have made up his music out of whole cloth. His blues do not follow traditional harmonic resolution; his vocals and his lyrics are often altogether and strikingly original; and, though the influence of Blind Lemon Jefferson and Peetie Wheatstraw can be discerned, it comes as a shock, after all the familiar blues figures, to hear his jagged music, the rapidly picked notes and eccentric rhythms, the start-and-stop-and-start-again of its energies, the brilliant flights of improvisation, and the denial of melodic resolution. "Robert Pete Williams fulfills a unique condition in blues," wrote Alan Wilson of the rock and boogie group, Canned Heat, "one which other [blues singers] merely hint at: a musical style in which improvisation plays nearly as important a role as pre-determined factors."

Duke Records

Finally, at the opposite end of the blues spectrum, Houston's Duke and Peacock Records, owned by Don Robey (a light-skinned black man who was reputed to be a numbers boss and first got into the record business through his nightclub, the Bronze Peacock), played as big a part as any independent label both in disseminating the new style of blues and in changing the old throughout the South. Although a few downhome sides came out on the label, it was the squalling brass, T-Bone Walker-styled guitar, and big band arrangements of Joe Scott, an inspired orchestrator and producer, that best characterized the Duke/Peacock sound. For the most part, this was a whole different kind of blues than is being discussed in this book—

an outgrowth of the jump and blues ballad styles of the late 1940s and an intermediate step on the way to soul. Certainly Duke was an all-purpose commercial recording company, serving up rock'n'roll, rhythm and blues, teen tunes, gospel, and sentimental ballads, not simply a diet of steady blues. However, there is no denying the blues content of their biggest hits. Duke may have provided Memphis exiles like Bobby "Blue" Bland and Junior Parker with more polished and jewel-like settings, but they never strayed far from their blues roots. Big Mama Thornton, who had a landmark hit with "Hound Dog" on the Peacock label in 1953, was one of the few women blues singers to carry on the tradition of Memphis Minnie. In addition, Duke recorded more obscure downhome artists like James Davis, Fenton Robinson, and Larry Davis, each of whom made several notable contemporary recordings that showed the same care and attention to detail that Duke lavished on its more elaborate productions.

Blues, then, was just something that wouldn't go away. It outstayed welcomes of fashion and commerce and outlived repeated predictions of its own demise. When I was growing up in Boston, the disc jockeys on Boston's black-oriented station, WILD, always announced a trip to Sam Jones's Basement—we're going way down in the alley, baby—whenever they put on a blues record. In every city, in every state, wherever there was a sizeable black population, the blues continued to surface and be recorded. In Boston, a record store owner named Skippy White formed his own label, Bluestown, to record a local barber named Alvin Hankerson, who was dubbed Guitar Nubbit because he was missing a couple of fingers on his right hand. Nubbit's records sold fairly well locally but became collector's items world-wide. In Chicago, little clubs spring up and little clubs fold with predictable irregularity, but there are always a couple of dozen spots in town to catch the blues, in whatever form or fashion may be in vogue. As late as 1970, Calvin Leavy had a big hit all through the South with "Cummins Prison Farm," a downhome take-off on the news of prison farm brutalities that sounds as if it was loosely modeled on Lightnin' Hopkins's "Tom Moore's Farm" of a couple of decades before. The blues can always surprise you, because it will never quite disappear. Just when you think it's gone and become another piece of nostalgia, it will spring back, stiff and proud and alive. As Rufus Thomas has said: "Blues will always be here. Words change, the style of music changes, of all the other music in the world, watch it—it'll tail out and always change. But you'll always be able to hear twelve-bar blues. Always. It's the backbone of American music—blues and country—everything else comes from that."

SELECTED RECORDINGS

GENERAL ANTHOLOGIES

■ **Home Again Blues (Mamlish)**

Subtitled "Really the Postwar Blues," this forms a complement to Origin's revelatory prewar blues series and is made up of songs recorded between 1946 and 1953 that have little in common except country roots and musical excellence. Luther Huff, Baby Face Leroy,

Hot Rod Happy—the blues roll on!
- **Mississippi Blues (United)**
- **Arkansas Blues (United)**

Recorded in the field by the Bihari brothers and their talent scout, Ike Turner, in 1951–1952. Many of the recordings on these albums remained unissued for nearly twenty years—and for good commercial reason. They are out of time and out of tune, full of a sense of life and good-humored self-confidence. It would be a mistake to try to sell these records on the basis of individual merit, but listen to the exuberance of these primitive band tracks and try to imagine them played in the little jook joints around Helena, Little Rock, and Clarksdale, Mississippi, where they must have sounded like a symphony.

NEW ORLEANS RHYTHM
INDIVIDUAL PERFORMERS

Professor Longhair
- **New Orleans Piano (Atlantic)**
- **Crawfish Fiesta (Alligator)**

The best of the eccentric Professor—among his first and last. The Atlantic sides date from 1949 and 1953 and could fairly be labeled classics, if it were not that the sobriety of such a designation is totally at odds with the inspired lunacy of the music. **Crawfish Fiesta**, recorded just before Longhair's death in early 1980, is no less surprising, no less engaging, but a little more flowing—simply because it is the result of a well-thought-out series of sessions rather than stemming from a thrown-together collection of singles. The rhythms start and stop according to some weird logic of their own, but here Professor Longhair, hailed as the Bach of Rock, really gets a chance to stretch out.

Smiley Lewis
- **I Hear You Knocking (English United Artists)**
- **The Bells Are Ringing (English United Artists)**

If you can't get these, any Smiley Lewis will do. Affable, expansive, a country Big Joe Turner, Smiley Lewis has never been accorded his rightful place in blues history. Here the balance should be redressed a little, with the inclusion of originals like "One Night," "I Hear You Knocking," "Shame Shame Shame," and "Blue Monday," all sung in Smiley's big-voiced, big-hearted, *smiley* way, with a stellar collection of New Orleans session men (including Fats Domino) behind him.

Guitar Slim
- **The Things That I Used to Do (Specialty)**

An essential record, not so much for Slim alone as for the change it marked in postwar blues. Here you have all the fervor of Mississippi blues mixed with gospel changes. Listen for Ray Charles on piano and Ray Charles's style in embryo; look out for telltale traces of Buddy Guy, the Carter Brothers, Albert Washington, and other equally histrionic vocalists, for this is where they got their inspiration.

Zydeco

Clifton Chenier and his Red Hot Louisiana Band
- **Louisiana Blues and Zydeco (Arhoolie)**
- **Bon Ton Roulet (Arhoolie)**

- **Clifton Chenier Live (Arhoolie)**
- **Bogalusa Boogie (Arhoolie)**

The full range of Clifton, from trio work—with just rubboard and drums accompanying his accordion on some selections on the first album—to full band accompaniment (including sax) on the last. There's no sound quite like zydeco, and within zydeco none quite like Clifton's, as the wheezing accordion takes on all the tonal coloration of Little Walter's harmonica, and then some, and a polite traditional music is transformed into piledriving rhythms and crazy, rocking good times. The first album is bluesiest, the first two most strongly traditional, but perhaps the best introduction is the live album, recorded at the kind of Creole dance in Richmond, California, where the good times start at dusk and can proceed without intermission until the sun comes up. From there you can go either backward or forward, to the early Specialty and Flyright (originally Zynn) albums or to **Bogalusa Boogie**, the sixth in a total of eight albums he has recorded so far for Arhoolie.

—— THE SWAMP SOUND OF LOUISIANA ——
—— ANTHOLOGIES ——

- **The Excello Story (Excello)**

Like the various Sun collections, this is not all blues by any means, but consists of rockabilly, rhythm and blues, and group sounds as well. The blues is great stuff, though a better collection could undoubtedly be put together. The overall impression is something of a hodgepodge, but some of the best of Lightnin' Slim, Slim Harpo, and Lonesome Sundown is still here.

- **Louisiana Blues (Arhoolie)**

A much better collection, featuring Silas Hogan and Whispering Smith from the Excello artists and Baton Rouge neighbors Guitar Kelley, Henry Gray, and Clarence Edwards as well. In a sense this documents the sound of local blues without the intervention of a commercial label like Excello. The heavy, doomy sound often remarked upon in discussions of Excello is very much in evidence here, with Clarence Edwards (who appeared on the magnificent **Country Negro Jam Session**) singing in the dark tones of Howlin' Wolf, Guitar Kelley sounding very much like local kingpin Lightnin' Slim, and the effect of the whole very much like what the best Excello records have been—but without the commercial overlay.

—— INDIVIDUAL ARTISTS ——

Lightnin' Slim
- **Rooster Blues (Excello)**
- **The Early Years (Flyright)**
- **Trip to Chicago (Flyright)**

The first, containing many of his best known numbers, served for years as a kind of landmark of Slim's sound, heavy, plodding, and monotonous though it may have been. Lightnin' Slim sings with very little inflection and almost no changes of musical background, but his flat grainy voice remains effective at establishing mood and ambience. The latter two albums, with unissued alternate takes, rough early cuts, and improvised narratives, are actually much more interesting, almost surprisingly so; and although in some ways the practice of serving up alternate takes is a suspect one, here nothing is lost and a great deal is gained in the way of spontaneity.

Slim Harpo
■ Raining in My Heart (Excello)

Here it probably makes sense to stick to the tried and true—if you can find it—though there are a couple of Flyright albums similar to the Lightnin' Slim containing alternate takes and unissued cuts. Numbers like "I'm a King Bee" and "I Got Love If You Want It," "Raining in My Heart" and "Blues Hangover" are perfect just as they were, with that studied combination of art and artlessness—Slim's "put-on" nasal voice, the simplicity of his harmonica playing, and Jay Miller's uncluttered but calculated production. Lightweight, but lots of fun.

Silas Hogan
■ Trouble at Home (Excello)

Oddly enough a better record than either of the Excello efforts by Lightnin' Slim or Slim Harpo, though Hogan was by no means as significant an artist commercially or even aesthetically. There's a lot of Jimmy Reed here, but as on the Arhoolie anthology there's more of a sense of mood, a more somber unity, than on either of the Slim LPs. As Mike Leadbitter writes in the notes, "The inspiration behind the records of Silas Hogan was that of Lightnin' Slim . . . but where Slim draws on traditional material for his blues, Silas tried hard to be original and would sing his own songs with emotion and conviction." And here they are.

Lonesome Sundown
■ Been Gone Too Long (Alligator)

The very model of what a "rediscovery" blues album should be. Lonesome Sundown (Cornelius Green) here surpasses his previous output for Excello, recreating the Excello sound when called for but drawing upon a combination of resources—soul, blues, and rock'n'roll—far more original and varied than anything heard in his previous work. There are tremolo-laden Lightnin' Hopkins-styled blues; an occasional back-up chorus and horns are intelligently employed; and Sundown's melodic, easygoing vocals are adaptable to everything from hard blues to Brook Benton ballads. This is a record that is accessible to even the most recalcitrant non-blues enthusiast, but for me the high point comes in the final number, a blues (naturally), in which Sundown shouts out affably, "City girls hang out on Hope Street every shape and every size/ Well, they look like a million dollars, but I got two for twenty-five."

Robert Pete Williams
■ Angola Prisoners' Blues (Arhoolie)
■ Those Prison Blues (Arhoolie)
■ Robert Pete Williams and Snooks Eaglin (Fantasy: two-record set)

Very much of a ringer here. Robert Pete Williams is uncategorizable. These are country blues, pure but not at all simple. The first album contains Williams's much quoted, semi-improvised "Prisoner's Talking Blues," in which he declares, "Sometimes I feel like, baby, committin' suicide/ I got the nerve if I just had anything to do it with," among other prisoners' more conventional laments. The second album is all Robert Pete, featuring such intensely autobiographical numbers as "Pardon Denied Again" and "I'll Be Glad When I'm From Behind Iron Walls." Robert Pete's half of the third album, a two-record set, was originally called **Free Again** and stems from his release from prison. This is no *easier* an album to listen to—and no less profound. Amid such songs as "Almost Dead Blues" and "Death Blues," he declares, in "I've Grown So Ugly," "I walked to the mirror for to comb my hair/ I made a move, didn't know what to do/ I done got so ugly, I don't even know myself." The guitar playing is as singular as the lyrics, jagged, rambling, wide-ranging, free. This is hard, uncompromising music, but it is as rewarding as anything in the blues, as the most difficult modern poetry. Place these albums—or at least one of them—on your list of indispensable items.

── DUKE RECORDS IN HOUSTON ──

Presently there is no good anthology of Duke material. Both Rounder and Ace Records have announced plans for Duke sets, but for now you'll have to stick to records by individual artists.

Clarence "Gatemouth" Brown
■ San Antonio Ballbuster (Charly)

The best of Gatemouth's Duke sides, 1949–1956, this is a very enjoyable album from one of T-Bone Walker's more imaginative disciples. Gatemouth Brown is a dirtier singer and a funkier instrumentalist than his mentor, with country-and-western roots and an equal facility on guitar, harmonica, and fiddle. Here he plays nothing but the blues, tearing along in fine fashion and getting down in the alley, too, adapting T-Bone's slick urban style to Duke's loping Texas beat and coming up with a mix that is convincing and ingratiating at the same time. This is the kind of record that, without ever aspiring to high art, rewards repeated listening and yields new pleasures time and time again.

Big Mama Thornton
■ Big Mama Thornton in Europe (Arhoolie)

Once again Arhoolie comes through with a record that both sums up a career and extends our appreciation for an otherwise marginal artist. Big Mama's Duke sides, including the original of "Hound Dog," come across as somewhat stiff and dated, but here she breaks free with magnificent and varied support from a band that includes Buddy Guy and Walter Horton, and on solo sides with Fred McDowell backing her on slide guitar. "Hound Dog," "Little Red Rooster," and "Sweet Little Angel" have never sounded better, and you can really understand what it was about Big Mama—more than just her buzz-saw voice and commanding girth and presence—that made her the logical successor to Memphis Minnie.

Junior Parker
■ Junior Parker: The ABC Collection (ABC/MCA)
■ I Tell Stories Sad and True (United Artists)

This is the mature Junior (no longer Little Junior) Parker. You miss the youthful exuberance of his Memphis sides, but the performances here are masterfully self-assured. **The ABC Collection** is a good overview of the Duke sides, not the most obvious commercial hits. An eloquent use of phrasing and silence, both in the vocals and the harmonica playing. On the United Artists album, cut in 1972, Parker really stretches out, with a gréat six-minute version of Willie Nelson's "Funny How Time Slips Away," complete with dramatic monologue, and affecting interpretations of classic Percy Mayfield, Roy Brown, and Guitar Slim material. Junior Parker projected a kind of classiness in a way that few blues singers have managed to do without seeming pretentious. Also, like only a few artists in any field, his work seemed to get better and more complex right up until his premature death at thirty-nine in 1971.

Bobby "Blue" Bland
- **Here's the Man (Duke/MCA)**
- **Two Steps From the Blues (Duke/MCA)**
- **Call on Me (Duke/MCA)**
- **Ain't Nothing You Can Do (Duke/MCA)**
- **Introspective of the Early Years (Duke/MCA)**

An underrated performer. Along with Sam Cooke and Ray Charles, Bland was a forerunner of·the modern soul movement; but, perhaps because he did not play an instrument or write his own songs, he was for years seen as a mechanical kind of stylist, a stand-up singer who was placed in front of the band and given directions as to how to perform. This is not at all the case. As much as Charles or Cooke, Bobby Bland created a very personal style, a mix of gospel and blues that was both charismatic and deeply felt. These albums represent his best and most influential sides, with intricate big band arrangements, a thoughtful reading of lyrics that are often "deep" and sometimes profound, and vocals that orchestrate both the silky qualities of Bland's voice and the rough gospel scrawk that became his trademark. The **Introspective** is a quirky selection of some of his better early sides, but the three individual albums—from which the collection draws to some extent—are indispensable.

APPENDIX

Where to Buy Blues Records

The records that are available in this book are for the most part not going to be available in your average local record store. This is because the major labels have almost entirely gotten out of the blues business. The result is that if you don't have an exceptional specialist store near you, the easiest way to purchase blues records is through the mail. The largest mail order store that I know, which puts out its own comprehensive blues catalogue, is Down Home Music, 10341 San Pablo Ave., El Cerrito, California 94530. In the midwest the Jazz Record Mart—at 11 West Grand, Chicago, Illinois 60610—does a great deal of mail order business. In the east Round Up—at Box 147, Cambridge, Mass. 02141—carries nearly all the blues labels, and Cheapo—at 645 Mass. Ave., Cambridge, Mass. 02139—offers an exceptional selection of blues in their walk-in store. In England Bill Millar tells me the most extensive selection of blues records is available through Red Lick Records in Hendy, Ynsfor, Llanfrothen, Penrhyn, Gwynedd, Wales.

BLUES PERIODICALS

Living Blues, 2615 North Wilton Ave., Chicago, Illinois 60614.
Blues Unlimited, 36 Belmont Park, Lewisham, London, England.

Both are quarterlies, more or less. *Blues Unlimited* goes back to 1963; *Living Blues* started in this country in 1970. An enormous amount of the scholarship and blues detective work that has taken place over the last twenty years has been the result of the efforts of these two magazines, propelled by sheer enthusiasm rather than by any financial grants or academic discipline. If you want to find out what's going on in the blues, check out both.